Best Home
BAKING

The Old Farmer's Almanac

Best Home
BAKING

Irresistible Recipes from
America's Blue Ribbon Bakers

The Old Farmer's Almanac Books
Series Editor: Sarah Elder Hale
Consulting Editor: Susan Peery
Copy Editor: Barbara Jatkola
Proofreader: Jack Burnett
Art Director: Carol O. Loria
Illustrations, pp. 73, 105: Karen Savary

Cover illustration and chapter title page art:
Warren Kimble®

Distributed in the book trade by Houghton Mifflin

The Old Farmer's Almanac®, North America's oldest continuously published periodical and the original Farmer's Almanac since 1792, is owned and published by:

Yankee Publishing Inc.
1121 Main Street
Dublin, NH 03444

For additional information about *The Old Farmer's Almanac,*
visit us on the Web at Almanac.com

Second edition

Contents

Foreword 9
Introduction 11
Preface: Judging Scorecards 13

Chapter 1 Yeast Breads & Rolls 15

Honey Whole-Wheat Bread • White Bread • Cornmeal Yeast Rolls •
Old-Fashioned Potato Bread • Wheat Germ Herb Bread • Onion Lovers' Bread •
Greek Anise Bread • Golden Pumpkin Raisin Bread • Sourdough Onion-Potato
Rye Bread with Caraway • Rye Bread • Dinner Rolls • Honey Oatmeal Bread •
Orange Bread • Cinnamon Rolls • Italian Easter Bread

How Yeast Works • The Mystery of Gluten • Baking with Rye Flour

Chapter 2 Quick Breads & Muffins 35

Cranberry-Orange Scones • Cranberry-Ginger Bread • Irish Bread • Cheddar
Cheese Pepper Bread • Date Bran Muffins • Michigan Cherry Muffins •
Zucchini Bread • Orange Nut Bread with Orange Cream Cheese Spread •
Banana Nut Bread • Great-Grandmother's Banana Bread • Irish Soda Bread •
Skillet Corn Bread • Spiced Pear Muffins

Pepper Power • Baking Soda & Baking Powder

Chapter 3 Coffeecakes **49**

Danish Nut Loaf • Apple-Walnut Poppy Seed Coffeecake • Sour Cream Coffeecake #1 • Orange Bowknot Rolls • Coffeecake Muffins • Apricot Tea Ring • Bavarian Coffeecake • Sour Cream Coffeecake #2

Save Some for Later • Freezing Baked Coffeecakes • Pan Size Substitutions

Chapter 4 Frosted Cakes **61**

Hungarian Nut Torte • Cream Cheese Cake • Moist Chocolate Cake with Cocoa Butter Frosting • Peanut Butter Chocolate Chip Cupcakes • Date and Walnut Cake • Chocolate Torte with Vanilla Sauce and Raspberries • Forest Chiffon Cake • Swiss Chocolate Cake • Nany's Caramel Peanut Butter Cake • Linzertorte Cake • White Cake with Coconut and Whipped Cream • Black Walnut Layer Cake • Chocolate Coconut Cream Cake • Pumpkin Cake • The Best Carrot Cake Ever • Gingerbread Cake • Apple-Walnut Celebration Cake • The Best Chocolate Birthday Cake • Zucchini-Yogurt Cake

All Flour Is Not Created Equal • Serving a Pretty Cake • Cake Flour: The Baker's Secret Ingredient • Toasting & Grinding Nuts • Is White Chocolate Really Chocolate? • Cracking the Coconut • The Elusive Black Walnut

Chapter 5 Unfrosted Cakes **91**

Coconut Cake • Orange Chiffon Cake • Cowboy Cobbler • Buttermilk Poppy Seed Cake • Perfect Pound Cake • Pearadise Tart • Plantation Pecan Cake • Cranberry and Pear Butter Crumb Cake • Pineapple Cheesecake • Chocolate Caramel-Pecan Cheesecake • Angel Food Cake • Banana Marble Pound Cake • Cherry Pudding Cake • Old-Fashioned Gingerbread • Raspberry-Lemon Pudding Cake • Quick Buttermilk Cake • The World's Best Cheesecake

Cream the Butter and Sugar Thoroughly • Peeling Peaches • The Pleasing Pecan • Zestier Lemon • Beating the Egg Whites into Shape • Cake-Baking

Chapter 6 Fruit Pies..**113**

A Great American Apple Pie • Blueberry Streusel Pie • Wild Blueberry Pie • Delicious Rhubarb Pie • Angie's Apple Crumb Pie • Peach Pie • Downeast Burgundy Berry Pie • Pear-Almond Pie • All-American Apple Pie • Schnappsy Peach Pie • Cherry Pie • Cranberry Pie • Ginger Peach Pie

The Perfect Cooking Apple • Wild Blueberries • Mace and Nutmeg

Chapter 7 Custard & Cream Pies...**129**

Coconut-Banana Cream Pie • Cranberry-Walnut Chess Pie • Pumpkin-Butterscotch Mousse Pie • Pecan Custard Pie • Chocolate-Rum Chiffon Pie • Lemon Sponge Pie • Coffee Cream Pie with Chocolate Crust • Irish Potato Pie • Sweet Potato Pecan Pie • Lemon Meringue Pie • Date Delight • Pumpkin Pie • Southern Sweet Potato Pie

Chapter 8 *Bars & Brownies*...143

Pumpkin Cheesecake Bars • Lemony Hazelnut Bars • Triple-Good Bars •
Peanut Butter Bars • Decadent Brownies • Apricot-Almond Bars • Caramel
Rocky Road Bars • Yam-Oatmeal Squares • The World's Best Brownies •
Cherry-Filled White Chocolate Bars • Cream Cheese Swirl Brownies

Chapter 9 *Cookies*...155

Cranberry-Coconut Cookies with Toffee • Empire Biscuits • Triple-Peanut
Cookies • Chocolate-Orange Delights • Apple-Toffee Cookies • Chocolate
Peppermint Creams • Sima's Yummy Rugelach • Molasses Cookies •
German Hazelnut Cookies • Triple-Treat Peanut Butter Chocolate Chip Cookies •
Raspberry-Orange Mazurkas • White Chip Chocolate Cookies • Grandma's Best
Butter Cookies • Orange Citrus Cookies • Cherry Thumbprints •
Zucchini Drop Cookies

Chopping Dried Fruit • Cinnamon • Don't Discard Those Egg Whites!

Chapter 10 *Too Good to Leave Out*...173

Blueberry Bread Pudding • Apple Dumplings • German Apple Pancakes •
Zucchini Pizza • Gougères • Blueberry Oatmeal Crisp • Cream of Tartar
Biscuits

Appendix: List of Fairs, Festivals, & Bake-offs...181

Index...185

Foreword

THE OLD FARMER'S ALMANAC, NOW IN ITS FOURTH CENTURY of publication, has always concerned itself with the basics of daily life, from the predictable movements of the Sun, the Moon, and other heavenly bodies to the weather (less predictable), household advice, gardening, and food. To be honest, though, it's only in the past half century or so that food and recipes have played a big role.

The founder of the Almanac and its editor for the first 54 years, Robert B. Thomas (1766–1846), left us only slight evidence of his culinary tastes. For instance, he recommends in his 1834 Almanac what he considered to be a superior way of roasting potatoes in the fireplace: Wrap the potatoes individually in several layers of paper, soak them in water, and then cook them in hot ashes until the paper dries out and the potatoes are done.

This is not to say that cooking was unimportant in those days. A contemporary of Thomas, the French gastronome Brillat-Savarin, declared that the ". . . discovery of a new dish does more for human happiness than the discovery of a new star." We venture to suggest, however, that Thomas, who had studied almanac-making at a special school in Boston and who made all his own astronomical calculations, would have cast his lot with the new star.

We still have reams of astronomical calculations in *The Old Farmer's Almanac*, but over the years food and cooking have grown in importance. Each issue of the Almanac contains a food feature, the vegetable gardening stories often include recipes, and then there is the reader recipe contest, which attracts hundreds of entries every year from the United States and Canada. The editorial staff evaluates and tests all of the contest recipes—and that includes tasting them (well . . . devouring them, in some cases!). Most of all, we want the food to taste good and look good.

This book is devoted to home baking, my favorite form of cookery and one of the most satisfying. The smells and tastes of homemade baked goods linger in our memories. Who doesn't have a recollection of a special birthday cake, a sweet shared with a loved one, or a surprise contribution to a potluck supper? (We know of one to which everyone brought dessert!)

As far as food goes, we've come a long way from Robert B. Thomas's "recipe" for fireplace potatoes. On the other hand, with a little salt, pepper, and butter, they might be quite good.

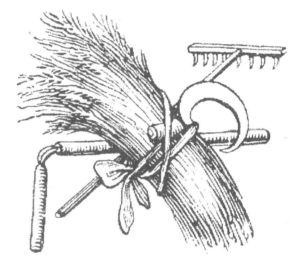

Susan Peery
The Old Farmer's Almanac
Dublin, New Hampshire

Introduction

I N YOUR HANDS IS A BOOK THAT IS A SEQUEL OF SORTS. *Best Home Baking* comes after my first book, *Blue Ribbon Recipes,* which evolved from my research on America's fairs and festivals for an article in *The Old Farmer's Almanac.* In the process of gathering recipes for two "blue ribbon" books, I have come to rely on the culinary arts directors, superintendents, and home arts administrators of fairs both large and small across the country. These are the people who responded enthusiastically to my initial call. They care deeply about good homemade food and the cooks who bring their dishes to fairs. They do everything from choosing judges to setting up tables, awarding ribbons, organizing volunteers, and speaking at schools and church groups to encourage youngsters to compete at fairs. They lament only one thing—that they never have a minute to enjoy the festivities. (I learned early on *not* to call during fair time!)

The culinary chairmen and chairwomen also are the liaisons between local cooks and corporate sponsors such as Softasilk, Land O' Lakes, Nestlé, Crisco, and Archway. And, most important for me, they are the connections between an editor and the recipes. They have mailed and faxed me hundreds of recipes, often with handwritten notes: "Yummy! Wins every year!" or "This cake tasted as good as it looked." Sometimes I learn about the cook: "She has exhibited every year for the past 25" or "Her mom won with this same recipe years ago." Without the generosity of these fair folks, I could not have uncovered the great recipes you'll find here.

For example, when I called Cathy Poluzzi, culinary chairwoman of the Dutchess County Fair in Rhinebeck, New York, she gave me more than 50 recipes from which to choose. At the Iowa State Fair (one of the country's oldest and largest), Arlette Hollister handpicked some favorites from the 7,000 food entries they receive each year, and we snatched up Ann McWilliam's Empire Biscuits (page 157). Our recipe tester agrees with Arlette—you'll not find a better shortbread recipe anywhere.

Speaking of our recipe tester, she is as much a contributor to this book as the fair directors and cooks. Kate Thomas of Fitzwilliam, New Hampshire, is one of the finest bakers we know. She has never officially studied cooking. In fact, she has a degree in Russian language and literature from Radcliffe. "My interest in baking began when I was ten," she says, "and was assigned bread making as a family chore. I think a part of why I cook so much is that I am a fussy eater and I know just what I want." Kate's pickiness is our gain. She tested for *Blue Ribbon Recipes,* and her comments were always precise and interesting.

Kate spent the better part of three months in her kitchen baking. She fed family, friends, and neighbors, making note of their opinions. Her best critics were husband Ben and sons Gareth and Gawain. Kate told me, "When the boys begged me to repeat a recipe, as in the case of Gawain's favorite, Coconut Cake [page 92], I knew we had a winner." When I called Kate to confer, I often heard the clanging of pots being washed in the background. She'd say, "Thank goodness for Ben; he does most of the cleanup." Ben had another important job—dropping off goodies at our office in Dublin on his way to his carpentry job. We'd see him coming and get a fresh pot of coffee going.

We hope you'll enjoy these delicious recipes as much as we have.

Polly Bannister
Editor

Postscript: Since this book was originally released in 1998, we have tested, tasted, and published in the Almanac, our calendars, and various other products an untold number of recipes for baked goods. The reissue of this cookbook provides an opportunity for us to share some of the best of these other recipes, which are the ones herein with no attribution—you can consider them yours!

Preface

Judging Scorecards

WE ALL REALIZE THAT TASTE IS SUBJECTIVE, and for this reason judging food is really quite difficult. Quantifying expressions such as "Yummy" and "Mmmmm," accompanied by vigorous head nodding, make the job of a food judge a real challenge. After years of experience, contest managers have developed rating systems that assign point values to important characteristics of dishes in competition. Point values may vary at each fair, but in general you'll find that flavor and appearance account for most of the score. To give you an idea of what judges look for in baked goods, here are some sample scorecards from the Ozark Empire Fair in Springfield, Missouri.

Yeast Breads
Flavor: Blend of well-baked ingredients, free from sourness	30
Texture: Tender, free from dryness or doughiness	25
Grain: Fine cells, evenly distributed	15
Crust: Uniform browning, free from cracks and bulges	15
Color: Characteristic of ingredients used, free from dark streaks	15

Quick Breads

Shape, Color, Volume: Well proportioned; evenly rounded or
flat top, depending on type of bread; uniformly brown;
light weight in proportion to size — 30

Crumb: Well raised and equally light throughout;
moist, elastic, tender; medium-fine, round, even cells;
flaky lightness; no tunnels; not dry or soggy; nuts and fruit
evenly distributed — 30

Flavor: Blended flavor of well-baked ingredients;
free from flavor of fat, baking powder, or salt — 30

Crust: Crisp, usually rough surface; tender, thin, no cracks — 10

Cakes

Flavor: Delicate and pleasing, well blended — 35

Texture: Cakes with butter/shortening should be tender, moist,
light, and have fine, even cells; cakes without fat should be tender,
feathery, resilient, and have fine, even cells — 35

Appearance: *Shape:* straight sides, slightly rounded top;
crust: smooth, uniform color, not cracked or sticky;
frosting: glossy, smooth, not too thick, suitable for cake;
filling: minimum one-quarter inch, fluffy, good flavor suitable for cake — 30

Pies

Crust: Texture flaky and tender; flavor agreeable,
no strong taste of fat or salt — 40

Filling: Characteristic flavor, not over- or undersweetened or spiced;
consistency: custards thoroughly cooked, thick, and smooth, or
fruit thick, firm, yet tender, neither too juicy nor too dry;
meringue light, tender, slightly sweet, at least one-half-inch thick,
no shrinking or weeping — 40

Appearance: Color and shape — 20

Cookies

Flavor: Well blended, natural flavor of ingredients — 50

Texture: Tender, small, even cells, not crumbly or hard, consistent with
type of cookie; thin cookie, crisp; drop cookie, soft; bar cookie, moist — 30

Appearance: Shape regular, color uniform, free from darkened edges — 20

Chapter 1

Yeast Breads & Rolls

Honey Whole-Wheat Bread

2 loaves

The cook won "Best of Show" for this recipe, which the judges said looked as good as it tasted. Our recipe tester agreed wholeheartedly, saying that this bread has become a family favorite. For a tasty variation, try adding ¼ cup flaxseeds and ¼ cup sesame seeds.

> 4 cups whole-wheat flour, divided
> ½ cup nonfat powdered milk
> 1 tablespoon salt
> 2 packages (2 tablespoons) dry yeast
> 3 cups water
> ½ cup honey
> 2 tablespoons vegetable oil
> 3½ to 4 cups white flour
> Cornmeal

In a large mixer bowl, combine 3 cups of the whole-wheat flour, powdered milk, salt, and yeast. Mix well. Heat the water, honey, and vegetable oil until warm (115° to 120°F). Add the warm liquid to the dry ingredients and beat on low for 30 seconds, scraping the bowl constantly. Beat on medium for 3 minutes more. By hand, stir in the remaining 1 cup whole-wheat flour and enough of the white flour to make a moderately stiff dough. Turn out onto a floured surface and knead for about 5 minutes. Place in a greased bowl, cover, and let rise until doubled in bulk, 45 to 60 minutes.

Punch the dough down. Divide in half, cover, and let rest for 10 minutes. Grease two 9x5-inch pans and sprinkle with cornmeal. Shape the dough into 2 loaves and place in the pans. Cover and let rise until doubled in bulk, about 30 to 45 minutes.

Preheat the oven to 375°F. Bake for 30 to 35 minutes. Cool on wire racks for 10 minutes before removing from the pans.

Reverend Nancy S. Donnelly, Glen Gardner, New Jersey
Hunterdon County 4-H and Agricultural Fair, Flemington, New Jersey

White Bread

2 loaves

This is an excellent recipe for basic white bread. Everyone loves it straight out of the oven.

2 packages (2 tablespoons) dry yeast
2¼ cups warm water, divided
3 tablespoons sugar
1 tablespoon salt
2 tablespoons shortening or butter
6 to 7 cups flour, divided
Melted butter

In a large bowl, dissolve the yeast in ½ cup of the warm water. Stir in the remaining 1¾ cups water, sugar, salt, shortening or butter, and 3½ cups of the flour. Beat until smooth. (The electric mixer is a real help here.) Stir in enough of the remaining flour to make the dough easy to handle. Turn the dough out onto a lightly floured surface and knead until light and elastic. Place in a greased bowl, cover, and let rise until doubled in bulk, about 1 hour.

Punch the dough down and divide it in half. Shape into 2 loaves and place in greased loaf pans (either 9x5-inch or 8½x4½-inch). Brush lightly with melted butter, cover, and let rise until doubled in bulk, about 1 hour.

Preheat the oven to 425°F and bake for 25 to 30 minutes, or until the loaves are golden brown and sound hollow when tapped. Remove from the pans, brush the tops with more melted butter, and cool on wire racks.

Cathy Stark, Standfordville, New York
Dutchess County Fair, Rhinebeck, New York

BLUE RIBBON TIP

★ ★ ★ ★ ★

HOW YEAST WORKS

Fairgoing cooks who bake their bread on summer days recognize that dough can rise too fast during hot weather, resulting in big air bubbles in the dough. They must find a cooler place for their bread to rise. Bread that rises more slowly will be more finely textured and often better tasting than bread that has been rushed along.

Yeast differs from other leavening agents in that it is actually alive. Yeasts are tiny organisms that occur naturally; their spores are floating in the air we breathe. Yeast can be captured from the wild and cultivated simply by exposing flour and water to the air. This is the source of the well-known sourdough starters. Obviously, doing this could result in catching the spores of less desirable strains of yeast, not to mention the spores of molds. Hence the development of dry yeast. In this form, we can think of yeast as a seed. When moisture and warmth awaken it from its dormant state, it starts to digest, to excrete carbon dioxide, and to reproduce. It finds plenty of nutrients in the flour present in the dough. Many recipes jump-start the yeast by mixing it with a little sugar water before combining it with other ingredients, but this is not essential.

When the yeast excretes carbon dioxide, the bubbles of carbon dioxide are what puff the bread up to make it rise. However, in an environment containing too much carbon dioxide, the yeast shuts down. That is why we punch the dough down periodically—to release the carbon dioxide so that the yeast can resume its process of digestion, excretion, and reproduction. Yeast reproduces very fast, so each rising will take less time than the previous one because a larger number of organisms are taking part. When the bread is baked, the yeast is killed.

Cornmeal Yeast Rolls

1 dozen rolls

The cook won first prize with these rolls when she was a student at Byron Middle School. They are tasty and light like a white roll, but they have some whole grain for extra flavor. A first-rate recipe.

1¼ cups cornmeal
1 cup boiling water
1 package (1 tablespoon) dry yeast
½ cup warm water
¾ cup scalded milk, cooled to lukewarm
½ cup (1 stick) butter or margarine, melted
⅓ cup sugar
2 egg yolks, slightly beaten
2 teaspoons salt
4 to 5 cups flour

Combine the cornmeal and boiling water in a large bowl. Stir well and let stand for about 10 minutes. In a medium bowl, dissolve the yeast in the warm water. Let stand for 5 minutes. Add the milk, butter, sugar, egg yolks, and salt to the cornmeal; blend well. Gradually add the yeast mixture to the cornmeal mixture, stirring well. Slowly add enough flour to make a soft dough. Turn the dough out onto a lightly floured surface and knead until smooth and elastic, about 5 minutes. Place in a greased bowl, turning to grease the top. Cover and let rise in a warm place (85°F) for 1 hour, or until doubled in bulk.

Punch the dough down and shape into 12 round rolls. Place on a greased baking sheet, cover, and let rise until doubled in bulk, about 30 to 45 minutes. Preheat the oven to 425°F. Bake for 20 minutes, or until golden brown. Serve warm.

Amber Brook, Byron, Georgia
Georgia National Fair, Perry, Georgia

Old-Fashioned Potato Bread

2 loaves

Here is what our recipe tester had to say about this recipe: "Yummy, beautiful, a keeper."

> 2 cups warm water
> 2 packages (2 tablespoons) dry yeast
> ½ cup sugar
> 1 tablespoon salt
> 1 cup warm mashed potatoes (about 2 medium potatoes)
> ½ cup (1 stick) butter or margarine, softened
> 2 eggs
> 7 ½ cups flour, divided
> 3 tablespoons butter or margarine, divided
> Flour for dusting (optional)

Put the warm water in a large mixer bowl. Sprinkle with the yeast and stir until dissolved. Add the sugar and salt; stir until dissolved. Add the cooked mashed potatoes, softened butter, eggs, and 3½ cups of the flour. Beat on medium until smooth, about 2 minutes. Gradually add the remaining 4 cups flour, mixing with a wooden spoon or your hands until the dough is smooth and stiff enough to leave the sides of the bowl. (The dough will be soft.) Melt 1 tablespoon of the butter and spread it over the dough. Cover with a double thickness of aluminum foil or plastic wrap. Let rise in the refrigerator for about 2 hours, or until doubled in bulk. Punch the dough down. Cover and refrigerate overnight.

The next day, turn the dough out onto a lightly floured surface. Knead until smooth and elastic and blisters appear on the surface, about 10 minutes. Divide the dough in half and shape each half into a smooth ball about 6 inches in diameter. Place each in a lightly greased 9-inch round cake pan. Melt the remaining 2 tablespoons butter and brush over the dough. Cover with a kitchen towel and let rise in a warm place (85°F) until doubled in bulk, about 1½ to 2 hours.

Preheat the oven to 400°F. With a sharp knife, make 3 cuts crosswise in the surface of each loaf. Then make 3 cuts lengthwise to create a crisscross pattern. Bake for 40 to 45 minutes, or until the loaves are well browned and sound hollow when tapped. Remove from the pans and cool on wire racks. If desired, dust the tops lightly with flour before serving.

Mrs. Cloyce Hollis, Belleville, Wisconsin
The Old Farmer's Almanac *Recipe Contest, Dublin, New Hampshire*

For more recipes and kitchen tips, go to Almanac.com/food.

Wheat Germ Herb Bread

2 loaves

Mary Frances Scheetz lived in Canfield, Ohio, for 25 years before retiring to Florida. Before leaving her hometown, she won many blue ribbons for her breads. This herb-scented bread makes a delicious accompaniment to almost any meal. You might want to vary the herbs to complement your main dish: basil and oregano to go with Italian dishes, dill and rosemary to accompany fish.

5½ to 6½ cups flour, divided
2 packages (2 tablespoons) dry
    yeast
1 teaspoon salt
⅓ cup sugar
1 teaspoon dried thyme leaves,
    crushed
1 teaspoon dried marjoram leaves,
    crushed

1½ cups milk
½ cup water
½ cup (1 stick) butter or margarine
2 whole eggs
1 egg, separated
1⅓ cups plus 1 tablespoon wheat
    germ, divided

In a large mixer bowl, combine 3 cups of the flour, yeast, salt, sugar, thyme, and marjoram; mix well. In a saucepan, heat the milk, water, and butter until warm (the butter does not have to melt). Add to the flour mixture along with the 2 whole eggs and 1 egg yolk. Beat for 3 minutes. Gradually stir in 1⅓ cups of the wheat germ and enough of the remaining flour to make a soft dough. Knead on a floured surface until smooth and elastic, about 10 minutes. Place in a greased bowl, turning to grease the top. Cover and let rise until doubled in bulk, about 1 hour.

Punch the dough down and divide into quarters. Form each part into a rope and twist 2 together to make a loaf. Fold the ends in and place in a greased loaf pan (either 9x5-inch or 8½x4½-inch). Repeat with the other 2 pieces of dough. Cover and let rise for 30 to 40 minutes.

Preheat the oven to 350°F. Lightly brush the dough with the egg white and sprinkle with the remaining 1 tablespoon wheat germ. Bake for 35 to 40 minutes. Loosely cover with aluminum foil for the last 5 to 10 minutes of baking. Remove from the pans and cool on wire racks.

Mary Frances Scheetz, Fort Myers, Florida
Canfield Fair, Canfield, Ohio

Onion Lovers' Bread

1 loaf

Although this is not a true sourdough bread, the tangy starter gives it a delicious zip. The starter needs to be made a day ahead. This recipe won "Best of Show," and with good reason—it is both gorgeous and delicious.

Starter

- 2 cups flour
- 2 tablespoons sugar
- 1 tablespoon malt vinegar
- 1 tablespoon salt
- 1½ cups lukewarm water

Bread

- 1 package (1 tablespoon) dry yeast
- ¾ cup warm water, divided
- 1 cup starter
- ½ cup olive oil
- ½ cup milk
- 2 tablespoons honey
- 1½ teaspoons salt
- 1 egg
- 4 to 5 cups flour, divided

Filling

- ¼ cup (½ stick) butter
- 1 cup minced onion
- 2 large cloves garlic, minced
- ¼ cup freshly grated Parmesan cheese
- 2 tablespoons poppy seeds
- 1 teaspoon paprika

- 1 egg beaten with 1 tablespoon water

To make the starter, combine all the ingredients thoroughly. The mixture will be thick. Cover and let sit at least 24 hours before using. After using, replenish by adding equal amounts of warm water and flour plus 1 teaspoon sugar.

To make the bread, in a large bowl dissolve the yeast in ¼ cup of the warm water. Let stand until dissolved. Stir in the starter, oil, milk, remaining ½ cup water, honey, salt, and egg. Add 2 cups of the flour and mix thoroughly. Knead in enough of the remaining flour, 1 cup at a time, to produce a smooth, not sticky, dough. Rub the top of the dough with oil, place in a bowl, cover, and let rise until doubled in bulk.

To make the filling, while the bread is rising, heat the butter in a skillet and sauté the onion and garlic lightly. Remove from the heat and stir in the Parmesan cheese, poppy seeds, and paprika. Cool.

When the dough has risen, punch it down and let it rest for 10 minutes. Roll out into an 18x12-inch rectangle and spread with the filling. Cut into 3 lengthwise strips. Carefully pinch together the edges of each strip to make 3 stuffed ropes of dough. On a greased baking sheet, loosely braid the ropes together and tuck the ends underneath. Cover and let rise for 30 to 40 minutes, or until doubled in bulk.

Preheat the oven to 375°F. Brush the dough with the egg-water mixture and bake for 35 to 40 minutes or until the loaf is golden brown and sounds hollow when tapped. Cool on the baking sheet for 10 minutes, then transfer to a wire rack to cool completely.

Vickie Medlin, Dallas, Texas
State Fair of Texas, Dallas, Texas

Greek Anise Bread

1 loaf

Here is another of Mary Frances Scheetz's blue ribbon winners.

- 1 package (1 tablespoon) active dry yeast
- ¼ cup warm water
- ⅓ cup sugar
- ¼ cup (½ stick) butter
- ½ teaspoon salt
- ½ cup milk, scalded
- ¼ teaspoon oil of anise
- 6 drops oil of cinnamon
- 3 cups flour (approximately), divided
- 1 egg
- 1 egg beaten with 1 tablespoon cold water
- 2 tablespoons sesame seeds

Soften the yeast in the water. Place the sugar, butter, and salt in a bowl and pour the hot milk over them. Stir until the butter melts. Cool to lukewarm. Stir in the oil of anise and oil of cinnamon. Add 1 cup of the flour. Mix well. Stir in the egg and softened yeast; beat well. Add enough of the remaining flour to make a soft dough. Turn out onto a lightly floured surface. Cover and let rest for 10 minutes.

Knead the dough until smooth and elastic, about 10 minutes. Place in a lightly oiled bowl, turning once to grease the surface. Cover and let rise until doubled in bulk, about 1¼ hours. Punch down and let rise again until almost doubled in bulk, about 1 hour.

Turn the dough out onto a floured surface and divide into 3 balls. Cover and let rest for 10 minutes. Roll each ball into a strand about 16 inches long, with tapered ends. Place the strands about 1 inch apart on a greased baking sheet. Braid loosely without stretching the dough, beginning in the middle and working toward either end. Pinch the ends together. Cover and let rise until doubled in bulk, about 40 minutes.

Preheat the oven to 375°F. Brush the dough with the egg-water mixture and sprinkle with the sesame seeds. Bake for 25 minutes, or until the loaf sounds hollow when tapped.

Mary Frances Scheetz, Fort Myers, Florida
Canfield Fair, Canfield, Ohio

Golden Pumpkin Raisin Bread

2 loaves

This sweet bread is sure to please.

- 2 packages (2 tablespoons) dry yeast
- ½ cup sugar
- ⅔ cup warm water
- 1 can (16 ounces) solid-pack pumpkin
- ¼ cup vegetable oil
- 2 teaspoons salt
- 2 teaspoons ground cinnamon
- 1½ teaspoons ground ginger
- ½ teaspoon ground nutmeg
- 6¼ to 7¼ cups flour, divided
- 2 eggs
- 1½ cups raisins

In a large bowl, sprinkle the yeast and sugar over the warm water; stir until dissolved. Add the pumpkin, oil, salt, cinnamon, ginger, nutmeg, and 1½ cups of the flour. Using a mixer on low speed, beat until well blended. Increase the mixer speed to medium and beat for 2 minutes more. Add the eggs and 1 cup flour; beat for 2 minutes. Stir in the raisins and enough of the remaining flour to make a moderately soft dough. Turn out onto a lightly floured surface. Knead until smooth and elastic, about 5 to 8 minutes. Place in a large greased bowl, turning the dough so that the top is greased. Cover with a kitchen towel and let rise in a warm place until doubled in bulk, about 1 hour. Note that because of the high sugar content, it is essential that the first rising be in a warm place; room temperature will not do. For the best results, put the bowl in a 125°F oven for 20 minutes to get things going.

Punch the dough down and divide it in half. Let rest for 10 minutes. Shape each half into a loaf. Place each loaf in a greased 9x5-inch pan. Cover and let rise until doubled in bulk, about 45 minutes.

Preheat the oven to 375°F. Bake for 35 to 40 minutes, or until the loaves are golden brown and sound hollow when tapped. Remove from the pans and cool on wire racks.

Stephanie Leach, Los Gatos, California
The Old Farmer's Almanac *Recipe Contest, Dublin, New Hampshire*

Sourdough Onion-Potato Rye Bread with Caraway

3 loaves

Paul was a member of the Poughkeepsie Police Department for 35 years, during which time he never baked. After retiring, he took an adult education course in breadmaking taught by a student at the Culinary Institute of America. His bread received awards at several fairs and was always a "winner" at his family celebrations and local church get-togethers.

Making a real sourdough bread is a whole new adventure for many cooks. This recipe is fun to make, and even though it appears complicated, it really isn't. While making the starter (rye sour), you may feel like an alchemist, and the people eating the delicious, moist slices will surely think that you have been working magic.

Rye Sour

2½ cups rye flour, divided
⅓ teaspoon dry yeast
2½ cups warm water, divided
1 tablespoon caraway seeds, crushed or ground in a coffee grinder
½ medium onion, minced
1½ cups white flour, divided

Filling

½ medium onion, minced
2 teaspoons caraway seeds
2 teaspoons olive oil
Dash of salt

Bread

2 medium potatoes (1 cup mashed)
2 packages (2 tablespoons) dry yeast
6 cups white flour (approximately), divided
1½ tablespoons salt
4 to 5 tablespoons caraway seeds
Cornmeal or vegetable cooking spray

¼ cup cold water
1 tablespoon cornstarch
1 cup boiling water

Begin making the rye sour 48 hours in advance. Combine ½ cup of the rye flour, yeast, 1 cup of the warm water, caraway seeds, and onion in a medium bowl and mix until smooth. The mixture should be soupy. Cover and let stand for 24 hours in a warm spot.

The next day, add 1¼ cups rye flour and ½ cup warm water. Stir until well blended and sprinkle the top with ¼ cup rye flour. Cover for 4 to 8 hours, or until the floured top appears cracked with fissures spread widely apart. Avoid letting the sour collapse. Add ¾ cup of the white flour and ½ cup warm water. Stir until well blended and sprinkle with ¼ cup rye flour. Let rise for 4 to 8 hours, or until fissures form. Add the remaining ¾ cup white flour and remaining ½ cup warm water. Stir and sprinkle with the remaining ¼ cup rye flour and let rise for another 4 to 8 hours.

To make the filling, combine all the ingredients in a small bowl and set aside.

To make the bread, cook the potatoes and drain, reserving 1 cup of the cooking water. Mash the potatoes. In a large bowl, dissolve the yeast in the warm potato water (105° to 120°F). When bubbles start to form, blend in the mashed potatoes and rye sour. Add 3 cups of the white flour, salt, and caraway seeds. Mix with a wooden spoon until the dough pulls away from the sides of the bowl, adding up to 3 more cups flour as needed. Turn the dough out onto a floured surface and knead for about 5 to 8 minutes. Knead in the filling and enough flour to make a soft, slightly sticky dough. Place the dough on an oiled surface, cover, and let rest for 15 minutes.

Preheat the oven to 200°F. Divide the dough into 3 parts. Either shape into round loaves and place on baking sheets sprinkled with cornmeal or place in loaf pans coated with vegetable cooking spray. Place in the oven, turn the temperature off, and leave the door open while the loaves rise for about 45 minutes. Remove from the oven, then preheat the oven to 375°F. Place an empty baking pan (about 10x8 inches) on the lower rack of the oven while it is heating.

Meanwhile, in a small bowl, combine the cold water and cornstarch. Add the boiling water and stir. With a pastry brush, coat the dough with the cornstarch mixture. Poke about 12 holes in each loaf with a skewer or peeled stick. Put about a dozen ice cubes in the baking pan and bake the loaves for 35 to 40 minutes, or until they sound hollow when tapped. Turn out onto wire racks, brush again with the cornstarch solution, and cool.

Paul C. Osterman, Poughkeepsie, New York
Dutchess County Fair, Rhinebeck, New York

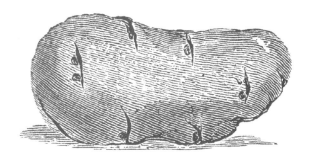

Rye Bread

2 loaves

- 1 cup milk
- 2 teaspoons salt
- 3 tablespoons shortening
- 3 tablespoons plus 1 teaspoon molasses, divided
- 1 package (1 tablespoon) dry yeast
- 1 cup warm water (110°F)
- 2 cups medium rye flour
- 3 to 4½ cups white flour, divided
- 1 egg white beaten with 1 tablespoon water

In the microwave oven, heat the milk, salt, shortening, and 3 tablespoons of the molasses for 1 minute. (You also may do this on the stovetop.) Pour into a large bowl and cool to lukewarm. Add the yeast and remaining 1 teaspoon molasses to the warm water. Stir and let proof for 10 minutes. Add the yeast mixture to the milk mixture and stir with a wire whisk. Add the rye flour and 2 cups of the white flour; stir with a wooden spoon. Continue adding white flour until the dough pulls away from the sides of the bowl. Turn the dough out onto a floured surface and knead for 10 minutes, adding white flour to prevent the dough from sticking to the surface. Place in a greased bowl, cover with plastic wrap, and let rise in a warm place until doubled in bulk, about 1 hour.

Punch the dough down and knead for about 30 seconds. Divide in half and let rest for 5 minutes. Form into 2 round loaves and place on a greased baking sheet. Cover with plastic wrap and let rise until doubled in bulk, about 30 minutes.

Preheat the oven to 350°F. Make 3 slashes in the top of each loaf and brush with the egg-water mixture. Bake for 35 to 45 minutes, or until the loaves sound hollow when tapped. Remove from the baking sheet and cool on wire racks.

David Oxley, Seattle, Washington
Western Washington Fair, Puyallup, Washington

BLUE RIBBON TIP

BAKING WITH RYE FLOUR

Rye flour comes in many forms. Paul Osterman (see Sourdough Onion-Potato Rye Bread with Caraway, page 26) uses white rye flour to make his bread and believes that it makes the best loaf. Our tester used dark rye, and it came out very well. Medium rye flour also will yield a tasty loaf. White rye and dark rye flours can be obtained from specialty baking shops or from health food stores. Unlike wheat flour, rye flour contains no gluten, so it does not make a chewy bread. Making a good rye bread is always a careful balancing act, requiring enough rye flour to get a good rye flavor and enough wheat flour to give it an elastic texture. Extra care in proofing, kneading, and rising conditions will help to compensate for some of the elasticity lost by using rye flour. Give the bread extra time to rise if it needs it, and help the wheat flour do its job by kneading the dough especially well.

Dinner Rolls

4 dozen rolls

Longtime baker Elaine Jonas guarantees that these perfect little rolls will disappear quickly.

1 cup water
⅓ cup honey
¼ cup (½ stick) butter or margarine
4½ to 5 cups bread flour, divided
1½ teaspoons salt
2 packages (2 tablespoons) dry yeast
3 eggs
3 tablespoons butter, softened
Melted butter

Heat the water, honey, and ¼ cup butter to 120° to 130°F. In a large bowl, blend 2 cups of the flour, salt, and yeast. Add the liquid and beat with an electric mixer on medium speed for 3 minutes. Beat in the eggs. Stir in enough of the remaining flour to make a soft dough. Turn out onto a floured surface and knead until smooth and elastic. Place in a greased bowl, cover, and let rise until doubled in bulk, about 1 hour.

Punch the dough down. Divide into 3 parts. Cover and let rest for 15 minutes. Roll each portion out into a 12-inch circle. Spread each round with 1 tablespoon of the softened butter. Cut each round into 16 wedges. Starting at the wide end, roll each wedge up. Place point side down on a greased baking sheet. Cover and let rise until doubled in bulk, about 30 minutes.

Preheat the oven to 375°F. Bake for 10 to 12 minutes. Immediately brush the tops of the rolls with melted butter.

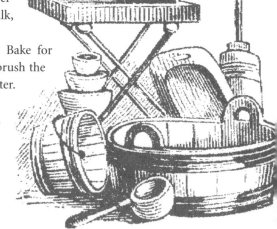

Elaine Janas, Columbia Heights,
   Minnesota
Minnesota State Fair,
   St. Paul, Minnesota

Honey Oatmeal Bread

2 loaves

5¾ to 6¼ cups flour, divided
2 packages (2 tablespoons) dry yeast
1¾ cups water
1 cup plus 6 tablespoons quick-cooking oats, divided
½ cup honey
1 tablespoon salt
⅓ cup butter-flavored shortening
2 eggs
1 egg white beaten with 1 tablespoon water
Oats for sprinkling

Combine 2 cups of the flour with the yeast in a large mixer bowl. In a saucepan, combine the water, 1 cup of the oats, honey, salt, and shortening. Heat until the shortening is almost melted. Cool to 110°F and add to the flour mixture. Add the eggs and beat on low for 30 seconds and then on high for 3 minutes. Using a wooden spoon, stir in as much flour as possible. Turn out onto a lightly floured surface and knead in enough of the remaining flour to make a moderately stiff dough that is smooth and elastic. Shape into a ball and place in a greased bowl, turning once to grease the top. Cover and let rise in a warm place until doubled in bulk, about 90 minutes.

Punch the dough down and turn out onto a lightly floured surface. Divide into 2 parts. Cover and let rest for 10 minutes. Grease two 9x5-inch pans. Sprinkle 3 tablespoons of the remaining oats into each pan. Shape the dough into loaves and place in the pans. Cover and let rise until doubled in bulk about 45 minutes.

Preheat the oven to 375°F. Brush the tops of the dough with the egg-water mixture. Sprinkle lightly with oats. Bake for 40 to 45 minutes. Cover loosely with aluminum foil during the last 15 minutes of baking to prevent overbrowning. Remove from the pans and cool on wire racks.

Sue Thomas, Indianapolis, Indiana
Indiana State Fair, Indianapolis, Indiana

Orange Bread

2 loaves

This tasty sweet bread goes perfectly with tea or coffee.

1¼ cups water
½ cup powdered milk
½ cup sugar
½ cup (1 stick) butter
Grated rind of 1 orange
½ teaspoon ground ginger
2 teaspoons salt
5 cups flour, divided
2 packages (2 tablespoons) dry yeast
2 eggs
1½ cups golden raisins
1 cup confectioners' sugar
½ cup walnuts, finely chopped
4 to 6 tablespoons orange juice

Place the water, milk, sugar, butter, orange rind, ginger, and salt in a saucepan and heat to 110° to 120°F. Place 2½ cups of the flour and the yeast in a large bowl. Pour the warm liquid over the flour and yeast and mix well. Add the eggs and raisins. Add the remaining 2½ cups flour and mix well. Turn out onto a lightly floured surface and knead until soft and elastic. Place in a greased bowl, cover, and let rise until doubled in bulk, about 1 hour.

Knead the dough and divide into 2 parts. Shape each into a loaf and place in a greased 8½x4½-inch pan. Cover and let rise until doubled in bulk, about 30 minutes.

Preheat the oven to 350°F. Make 3 shallow slits in the top of each loaf. Bake for 30 minutes, or until golden brown. Remove from the pans and cool on wire racks.

Meanwhile, mix together the confectioners' sugar, walnuts, and enough orange juice to make a fairly thick glaze. Spoon gently over the warm loaves.

Kathleen Shangraw, Huntington, Vermont
Champlain Valley Fair and Exposition, Essex Junction, Vermont

Cinnamon Rolls

dozen rolls

Dough

2 cups milk
½ cup brown sugar
1 package (1 tablespoon) dry yeast
1 cup rolled oats
5 to 6 cups bread flour
    (or all-purpose flour)
2 eggs, beaten
1 tablespoon salt
1 cup (2 sticks) softened butter,
    divided

Filling

¾ cup walnuts, chopped
½ cup raisins (optional)
1 cup sugar mixed with
    1 tablespoon cinnamon,
    divided
1 egg yolk, beaten

Icing

3 tablespoons butter, melted
1½ cups confectioners' sugar
1 to 2 tablespoons cream
Vanilla extract
Pinch of salt

Heat the milk slightly (to lukewarm). In a large bowl, combine the milk, brown sugar, yeast, rolled oats, and enough flour (1½ to 2 cups) to make a sponge the consistency of bubbly pancake batter. Set aside for a while (about 20 minutes) to allow the yeast to work. Then add the eggs, salt, and ½ cup of the softened butter. Stir well. Add the rest of the flour and knead into a soft dough. (Add the last cup while kneading, if you wish.)

Let the dough rise in a large buttered bowl covered with a damp towel, until it has doubled in size, at least 1 hour. Divide the dough into 2 pieces, and roll them out into 2 flat rectangles about ½ inch thick, 12 to 15 inches long, and 10 inches wide. Spread the remaining ½ cup softened butter onto the rectangles. Distribute walnuts and raisins (if using) evenly, and sprinkle with most of the cinnamon sugar. Roll up the dough the long way and pinch it shut. Slice each roll of dough into 12 pinwheel pieces, brush with egg yolk, and sprinkle with remaining cinnamon sugar.

Fit the rolls into 1 or 2 buttered round or rectangular pans (use whatever you have on hand; the rolls can be squeezed in or given lots of room), and let them rise again until they're puffy and doubled, about 45 minutes to an hour.

Preheat the oven to 350°F. Bake rolls for 25 to 30 minutes, or until they are cooked through and lightly browned. While they're still warm, spread icing on top.

Italian Easter Bread

1 loaf

Bread

¼ cup sugar
1 teaspoon salt
1 package (1 tablespoon) dry yeast
2½ to 3½ cups unbleached flour, divided
⅔ cups milk
2 tablespoons butter
2 eggs, at room temperature
½ cup chopped, mixed, candied fruit

⅓ cup chopped blanched almonds
½ teaspoon aniseed
2 tablespoons melted shortening
5 uncooked eggs, colored with Easter egg dye

Icing

1 cup confectioners' sugar
1 tablespoon milk
⅛ teaspoon vanilla extract

Colored sprinkles, for decoration

In a large mixing bowl, blend the sugar, salt, and yeast well with 1 cup of the flour. In a saucepan, combine milk and butter, heating slowly until liquid is warm and butter is melted. Pour the milk into the dry ingredients and beat 125 strokes with a wooden spoon. Add the two eggs and ½ cup flour or enough to make a thick batter. Beat vigorously for 2 minutes. Stir in enough more flour to make a ball of dough that draws away from the sides of the bowl.

Turn out onto a floured board and knead for about 10 minutes, working in additional flour to overcome stickiness. Place the dough into a greased bowl, turning to grease the top. Cover tightly with plastic wrap and put into a warm, draft-free place until doubled in bulk, about 1 hour. Meanwhile, combine the fruit, nuts, and aniseed.

Punch down the dough and return it to a lightly floured board. Knead in the fruit mixture, keeping the syrupy pieces dusted with flour until they are worked into the dough. Divide the dough in half. Carefully roll each piece into a 24-inch rope—the fruit and nuts will make this slightly difficult. Loosely twist the 2 ropes together and form them into a ring on a greased baking sheet. Pinch the ends together well. Brush the dough with melted shortening. Open up the twist slightly to make a place for each colored egg. Carefully push the eggs down into the dough as far as possible. Cover the bread with waxed paper and let rise in a warm, draft-free place until doubled in bulk, about 1 hour.

Preheat the oven to 350°F. Bake the bread for about 35 minutes, or until a toothpick inserted into a twist comes out clean. Place onto a wire rack to cool. Once the bread is cool, drizzle the icing on top between the eggs, and decorate with colored sprinkles.

Chapter 2

Quick Breads & Muffins

Cranberry-Orange Scones

8 scones

This is the kind of recipe you'll make again and again because it is so easy and so good. Dried cranberries can be found in many supermarkets under the name "Craisins" and in most health food stores. You may use them in place of raisins in many recipes. Try them in oatmeal, too.

2 cups flour
1 tablespoon baking powder
½ teaspoon baking soda
¼ teaspoon salt
3 tablespoons sugar, divided
1 tablespoon grated orange rind
½ cup (1 stick) cold butter, cut up
⅔ cup buttermilk
1 cup dried cranberries
1 tablespoon milk

Preheat the oven to 425°F. Combine the flour, baking powder, baking soda, salt, 2 tablespoons of the sugar, and orange rind in a bowl or food processor. Cut in the butter with a pastry blender or food processor. Stir in the buttermilk and dried cranberries, mixing just until moistened. Turn the dough out onto a lightly floured surface. Knead 5 or 6 times. Pat into an 8-inch circle. Cut into 8 wedges and place 1 inch apart on a lightly greased baking sheet. Brush with the milk and sprinkle with the remaining 1 tablespoon sugar. Bake for 15 minutes, or until golden brown. Remove from the pan and cool on wire racks.

Diana Ferris, Red Hook, New York
Dutchess County Fair, Rhinebeck, New York

Cranberry-Ginger Bread

1 loaf

The lime juice and ginger make this batter smell delicious, and the end result is a very good, very different, cranberry loaf. Our recipe tester says that next time she tries this recipe, she might use a little more lime juice and ginger and reduce the water proportionately.

2 cups flour
¾ cup sugar
1½ teaspoons baking powder
¾ teaspoon salt
½ teaspoon baking soda
¼ cup (½ stick) butter or margarine
1 teaspoon grated lime rind
1½ teaspoons grated fresh ginger
1 tablespoon lime juice
¾ cup water
1 cup fresh cranberries, chopped
½ cup nuts, chopped

Preheat the oven to 350°F. Place the flour, sugar, baking powder, salt, and baking soda in a mixing bowl or food processor. Cut in the butter until crumbly. Stir in the lime rind, ginger, lime juice, and water just to moisten. Stir in the cranberries and nuts and pour into a greased 9x5-inch pan. Bake for 55 to 65 minutes, or until golden brown and a toothpick inserted in the center comes out clean. Cool in the pan on a wire rack for 5 minutes. Remove from the pan and cool completely on the rack. Wrap in plastic wrap and let sit overnight.

Victoria Steponaitis, Middlebury, Connecticut
Cranberry Harvest Festival, East Wareham, Massachusetts

Irish Bread

2 loaves

The caraway seeds and sugar in this bread are a surprisingly delightful combination. Melissa Bouchard began baking bread at the age of 7, and at age 13 she entered in competition five ethnic recipes she'd never made before. This one received a blue ribbon. It's delicious with a bowl of soup for supper.

- 1 cup raisins
- 1 cup milk
- 3½ to 4 cups flour, divided
- ½ cup (1 stick) butter or shortening
- 1 cup sugar
- 2 eggs
- 1 teaspoon salt
- 2 tablespoons baking powder
- 1 to 3 tablespoons caraway seeds

Preheat the oven to 350°F. Soak the raisins in the milk for a few minutes. Drain, reserving the milk, and dredge the raisins with ½ cup of the flour. Beat the butter, sugar, eggs, and reserved milk. Combine 3 cups of the flour with the salt, baking powder, and caraway seeds. Add the flour mixture to the butter mixture and mix well. Add enough of the remaining flour to make a stiff dough. Stir in the raisins. Pour the batter into 2 greased 8½ x 4½-inch pans. Bake for 45 minutes, or until a toothpick inserted in the center comes out clean. Remove the bread from the pans and cool on wire racks. Wrap in a kitchen towel to prevent the crust from hardening.

Melissa Bouchard, Coventry, Rhode Island
Washington County Fair, Saunderstown, Rhode Island

Cheddar Cheese Pepper Bread

1 loaf

½ cup (1 stick) butter
2½ cups flour
2½ teaspoons baking powder
1 to 1½ teaspoons freshly ground black
   pepper
¾ teaspoon baking soda
¾ teaspoon salt
2 cups (about 8 ounces) shredded sharp
   cheddar cheese
2 eggs
1 cup (8 ounces) plain yogurt

Preheat the oven to 375°F. Butter and flour a 9x5-inch pan. Melt the butter in a small saucepan over low heat; set aside to cool. Combine the flour, baking powder, black pepper, baking soda, and salt in a large bowl. Stir in the cheese. In a medium bowl, lightly beat the eggs. Stir in the yogurt and melted butter. Add to the flour mixture, stirring just until moistened. Spoon into the prepared pan. Bake for 35 minutes, or until golden brown and a toothpick inserted in the center comes out clean. Cool in the pan on a wire rack for 10 minutes, then remove from the pan. Serve warm or toasted.

Georgeann Frajkar, North Arlington, New Jersey
Hunterdon County 4-H and Agricultural Fair,
Flemington, New Jersey

★ ★ ★ ★ ★

PEPPER POWER

Pepper has had the greatest impact on world history of any spice. It was the search for pepper that motivated Christopher Columbus and other explorers to find new routes around the world, and pepper continues to far outsell all other spices. Peppercorns are the berries of the pepper plant and often are picked as soon as they appear on the vine. Look for tellicherry pepper, which is allowed to vine ripen and therefore grows larger and more tangy than other pepper.

Date Bran Muffins

1 dozen muffins

1¼ cups flour
3 teaspoons baking powder
½ teaspoon salt
½ cup sugar
3 cups 100% bran cereal (not flakes)
1¼ cups milk
1 egg
⅓ cup vegetable oil
1 cup dates, chopped

Preheat the oven to 400°F. Grease 12 muffin cups. Stir together the flour, baking powder, salt, and sugar; set aside. Combine the cereal and milk and let stand for 1 to 2 minutes. Add the egg and oil; beat well. Stir in the dates. Add the dry ingredients and stir to combine. Pour into the muffin cups and bake for 20 to 25 minutes, or until golden brown. Remove from the pan immediately. Serve warm or at room temperature.

Dorothy Dillon, Indio, California
National Date Festival, Indio, California

For more recipes and kitchen tips, go to Almanac.com/food.

Michigan Cherry Muffins

1 dozen muffins

These muffins have a great flavor and texture, and they are low in cholesterol, too!

Vegetable cooking spray
1 cup flour
¾ cup oat bran
⅔ cup sugar
1 tablespoon baking powder
½ teaspoon salt
¾ cup skim milk
½ cup nonfat plain yogurt
⅓ cup margarine, melted and cooled
2 egg whites, slightly beaten
1 teaspoon almond extract
¾ cup dried cherries, chopped
⅓ cup pecans, chopped
2 teaspoons grated lemon rind

Preheat the oven to 400°F. Spray 12 muffin cups with vegetable cooking spray. In a medium bowl, combine the flour, oat bran, sugar, baking powder, and salt; mix well. In another bowl, combine the milk, yogurt, margarine, egg whites, and almond extract. Add to the flour mixture, stirring just until moistened. Fold in the cherries, pecans, and lemon rind. Fill the muffin cups two-thirds full. Bake for 20 to 25 minutes, or until golden brown. Remove immediately from the pan. Serve warm or at room temperature.

Robin Giordano, Traverse City, Michigan
National Cherry Festival, Traverse City, Michigan

Zucchini Bread

2 loaves

3 eggs
2 cups sugar
1 cup oil
1 tablespoon vanilla extract
2 cups grated zucchini
3 cups flour
1 teaspoon baking soda
1 teaspoon salt
1 tablespoon ground cinnamon
¼ teaspoon baking powder
½ cup nuts, chopped
Cinnamon sugar

Preheat the oven to 350°F. Grease two 8½ x 4½-inch pans. In a large bowl, beat the eggs, sugar, oil, vanilla, and zucchini. Sift together the flour, baking soda, salt, cinnamon, and baking powder. Beat into the zucchini mixture. Stir in the nuts. Pour into the prepared pans and bake for 45 minutes, or until a toothpick inserted in the center comes out clean. Remove from the pans and cool on wire racks. Sprinkle cinnamon sugar over the tops of the warm loaves.

Sharon Nichols, Wellington, Kansas
Wheat Festival, Wellington, Kansas

Orange Nut Bread with Orange Cream Cheese Spread

3 small loaves

These teatime treats are a standard offering at the Governor's Inn in Ludlow, Vermont.

Bread

- 2 cups sifted flour
- ½ teaspoon salt
- 1 teaspoon baking powder
- ¼ teaspoon baking soda
- ⅔ cup granulated sugar
- ⅓ cup unsalted butter, softened
- 2 eggs
- 1 cup freshly squeezed orange juice, with pulp
- ½ teaspoon vanilla extract
- ½ teaspoon orange extract
- 1 cup walnuts, chopped

Spread

- 3 packages (8 ounces each) cream cheese
- 1 thin-skinned navel orange, cut into chunks
- 3 to 4 tablespoons confectioners' sugar

Preheat the oven to 350°F. Sift together the flour, salt, baking powder, and baking soda. In a separate bowl, cream the granulated sugar and butter, then beat in the eggs one at a time. Add the orange juice alternately with the flour mixture. Add the vanilla, orange extract, and walnuts; stir well. Pour into 3 well-greased 6x3½-inch pans. Bake for about 40 minutes, or until a toothpick inserted in the center comes out clean. Remove from the pans and cool on wire racks. Wrap in plastic wrap and chill well before slicing.

Meanwhile, using a food processor equipped with a steel blade, combine the cream cheese, orange chunks, and confectioners' sugar. Refrigerate for a few hours to blend the flavors. Slice the bread thinly and make little sandwiches using the orange spread.

Deedy Marble, Ludlow, Vermont
Great New England Food Festival, Boston, Massachusetts

Banana Nut Bread

1 loaf

It's hard to beat this bread for rich banana flavor.

- **2 cups flour**
- **1 teaspoon baking soda**
- **⅛ teaspoon salt**
- **½ cup vegetable oil**
- **1 cup sugar**
- **3 eggs, beaten**
- **3 medium ripe bananas, mashed**
- **2 tablespoons buttermilk**
- **1 cup nuts, chopped**

Preheat the oven to 350°F. Sift together the flour, baking soda, and salt. In another bowl, cream the oil and sugar. Add the eggs, bananas, and buttermilk; beat well. Stir into the dry ingredients, then stir in the nuts. Pour into a greased 9x5-inch pan. Bake for 1 hour, or until a toothpick inserted in the center comes out clean. Cool for 10 minutes in the pan, then remove from the pan and cool completely on a wire rack.

Tammy Reiss, Moore, Oklahoma
Oklahoma State Fair, Oklahoma City, Oklahoma

For more recipes and kitchen tips, go to Almanac.com/food.

Great-Grandmother's Banana Bread

1 loaf

- ½ cup (1 stick) butter, softened
- 1 cup sugar
- 2 eggs, beaten
- ½ cup sour cream
- 2 bananas, mashed
- 1 teaspoon vanilla extract
- 2 cups bread flour
- 2 teaspoons baking powder
- 1 teaspoon baking soda
- ½ cup chopped pecans

Preheat the oven to 350°F. Cream butter and sugar in a bowl until light and fluffy. Add eggs, sour cream, bananas, and vanilla; mix well. Combine flour, baking powder, and baking soda, and add to egg mixture; mix well. Stir in pecans. Pour into a greased 9x5-inch loaf pan. Bake for 55 minutes, or until loaf tests done.

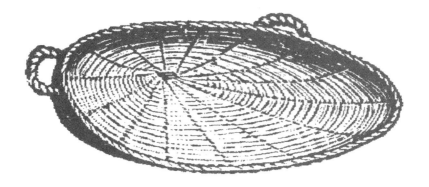

Irish Soda Bread

2 loaves

- **4 cups unbleached flour**
- **1 teaspoon salt**
- **1 tablespoon baking powder**
- **1 teaspoon baking soda**
- **¼ cup sugar**
- **⅛ teaspoon ground cardamom**
- **¼ cup (½ stick) butter**
- **1 egg, at room temperature**
- **1¾ cups buttermilk, at room temperature**
- **1½ cups currants**

Preheat the oven to 375°F. In a large bowl, combine the first six ingredients. Cut in the butter with a pastry blender or work it in with your fingers. Mix the egg and buttermilk together, then add this mixture to the dry ingredients. Stir until well blended. Add the currants and stir the mixture well. Turn out onto a floured surface and knead gently for 3 minutes, or until the dough is smooth.

Divide the dough into two pieces, shaping each into a round loaf. Place each into a greased 8-inch cake or pie pan, pressing it down until the dough fills the pan. Use a sharp knife to cut a ½-inch-deep cross on top of each loaf.

Bake for about 40 minutes, or until the bread sounds hollow when you thump it. Turn out onto a wire rack to cool. Do not cut for about 4 hours.

Skillet Corn Bread

6 to 8 servings

1 cup graham or whole-wheat flour
1 cup cornmeal
2 teaspoons baking powder
1 teaspoon baking soda
½ teaspoon salt
1⅓ cups buttermilk
2 eggs
¼ cup vegetable oil
¼ cup brown sugar

Preheat the oven to 400°F. Combine the flour, cornmeal, baking powder, baking soda, and salt in a medium bowl. In a separate bowl, whisk together the buttermilk, eggs, oil, and brown sugar until smooth. Add the buttermilk mixture to the flour mixture and stir just until blended. Pour into a greased 10-inch ovenproof skillet and bake for about 20 minutes, until golden brown and solid in the center. Serve warm.

Spiced Pear Muffins

12 muffins

- 1¾ cups flour
- 2 tablespoons sugar
- 1 teaspoon baking powder
- ½ teaspoon baking soda
- ½ teaspoon cinnamon
- ½ teaspoon ginger
- ½ teaspoon salt
- ¾ cup peeled, chopped fresh pears
- 1 cup buttermilk
- 3 tablespoons vegetable oil

Preheat the oven to 400°F. Grease a 12-cup muffin tin. In a bowl, stir together flour, sugar, baking powder, baking soda, cinnamon, ginger, and salt. Stir in pears, buttermilk, and oil; blend only until dry ingredients are moistened. Batter will be lumpy. Fill muffin cups ⅔ full and bake for about 15 minutes. Serve warm.

Chapter 3

Coffeecakes

Danish Nut Loaf

4 loaves

Light and yummy and not anywhere near as much work as these long instructions imply. Definitely a winner! (For tips on grinding nuts, see page 73.)

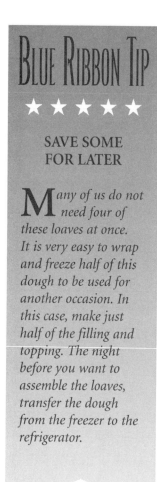

Dough

1 pound (4 sticks) butter, softened
4¾ cups flour, divided
2 packages (2 tablespoons) dry yeast
⅓ cup plus 1 teaspoon sugar, divided
½ cup warm water (105° to 115°F)
1 teaspoon salt
¾ cup milk (not skim)
2 eggs, slightly beaten

Filling

¼ cup honey
2 tablespoons butter or margarine
¼ cup milk
½ teaspoon vanilla extract
½ cup packed brown sugar
1 pound walnuts, ground

1 egg white, slightly beaten
¼ cup sugar
¼ cup ground walnuts

To make the dough, beat the butter and ½ cup of the flour together in a large bowl. (The electric mixer is helpful here.) Place the mixture between two sheets of wax paper. Roll out to a 12x10-inch rectangle. Place on a cookie sheet and refrigerate.

Sprinkle the yeast and 1 teaspoon of the sugar on the warm water. Stir and set aside until bubbly, about 10 minutes. In a large mixer bowl, combine the yeast

For more recipes and kitchen tips, go to Almanac.com/food.

mixture with 3 cups flour, the remaining ⅓ cup sugar, salt, milk, and eggs. Beat on medium for 3 minutes. Beat in the remaining 1¼ cups flour with a wooden spoon or with the dough hook of the electric mixer until the dough is shiny and elastic. (The dough will be soft.) Scrape down the sides of the bowl, cover with plastic wrap, and refrigerate for 30 minutes.

Turn the dough out onto a floured surface. Using flour as necessary to prevent sticking, roll out to a 22x14-inch rectangle. Peel the top sheet of wax paper off the butter mixture and place, butter side down, in the middle of the dough. Peel off the second sheet of paper and fold the uncovered dough over the butter to enclose it completely. Fold the dough in half, then in half again, making four layers. Sprinkle flour on any butter that may ooze out of the dough. Roll out to a 22x14-inch rectangle, using flour as necessary to prevent the dough from sticking. Repeat the folding and rolling 2 more times. If necessary, chill the dough between rollings. Place the dough in a large bowl. Cover tightly with plastic wrap and refrigerate overnight.

To make the filling, heat the honey, butter, and milk just until warm. Add the vanilla. Blend in the brown sugar and walnuts. (Do not do this a day ahead, or the consistency will not be right.)

Cut the dough into quarters. Roll one piece of dough out to a 12-inch square. (Making this piece really square will ensure a beautiful, even-looking loaf.) Keep the other pieces refrigerated. Cut the square into three 12x4-inch strips. Spread a scant ⅓ cup filling down the center of each strip. Roll up lengthwise, jelly roll–style. Place the 3 strips side by side and braid together. Tuck the loose ends underneath and gently place in a greased 8½x4½-inch pan. Repeat with the remaining dough. Let rise until doubled in bulk, about 45 minutes to 1 hour. (The dough will not reach the top of the pan.)

Preheat the oven to 375°F. Brush the dough with the beaten egg white. Combine the sugar and walnuts and sprinkle over the dough. Bake for 35 to 45 minutes, or until golden brown. Cool in the pans, then gently turn out onto wire racks.

Fran Hurayt, Austintown, Ohio
Canfield Fair, Canfield, Ohio

Apple-Walnut Poppy Seed Coffeecake

10 to 12 servings

Our recipe tester says, "This was quite good—a little better, I think, than the average sour cream coffeecake. The apples make it nice and moist, and it didn't last very long around my house."

½ cup vegetable oil
1 cup granulated sugar
2 eggs
1 teaspoon vanilla extract
2 cups flour
1 teaspoon baking powder
1 teaspoon baking soda
¼ teaspoon salt
3 tablespoons poppy seeds
1 cup sour cream
2 cups peeled, cored, and finely chopped apples
1 cup walnuts, chopped
¾ cup lightly packed brown sugar
1 teaspoon ground cinnamon
¼ cup (½ stick) butter, melted

Preheat the oven to 350°F. Grease and flour a 13x9-inch baking pan. Mix together the oil and granulated sugar. Beat in the eggs and vanilla; set aside. Sift together the flour, baking powder, baking soda, and salt. Stir in the poppy seeds. Add to the oil mixture alternately with the sour cream, beginning and ending with the flour mixture. Fold in the apples and pour into the prepared pan. Combine the nuts, brown sugar, cinnamon, and butter. Sprinkle over the batter. Bake for 35 to 45 minutes, or until a toothpick inserted in the center comes out clean. Cool in the pan for 10 minutes, then serve.

Julie DeMatteo, Clementon, New Jersey
The Old Farmer's Almanac *Recipe Contest, Dublin, New Hampshire*

Sour Cream Coffeecake #1

12 servings

Batter
- ½ cup (1 stick) butter
- 1 cup sugar
- 1 teaspoon vanilla extract
- 2 eggs
- 2 cups flour
- 1 teaspoon baking soda
- 1 teaspoon baking powder
- ½ teaspoon salt
- 1 teaspoon ground cinnamon
- 1 cup sour cream

Topping
- ½ cup chopped pecans
- 1½ teaspoons ground cinnamon
- ½ teaspoon vanilla extract
- ⅓ cup sugar

- 10 to 12 pecan halves

Preheat the oven to 350°F. Grease an angel food cake pan.

To make the batter, cream the butter and sugar. Add the vanilla and eggs and beat. Sift together the flour, baking soda, baking powder, salt, and cinnamon. Add to the butter mixture and mix well. Add the sour cream.

To make the topping, mix together all the ingredients.

Place the pecan halves neatly on the bottom of the prepared pan. Pour half of the batter into the pan and sprinkle half of the topping over it. Pour in the remaining batter and sprinkle with the remaining topping.

Bake for 40 to 45 minutes, or until a toothpick inserted in the cake comes out clean. Cool in pan, then turn onto serving plate.

Mary Schmaltz, Pueblo, Colorado
Colorado State Fair, Pueblo, Colorado

Orange Bowknot Rolls

24 rolls

Marjorie Johnson has loved baking since she was 8. She was one of six daughters and her mother's "best helper" when it came to the baking chores. Marjorie has won 2,447 ribbons in various competitions. These delicious rolls are light and not too sweet—great for weekend company.

Rolls

1¼ cups warm water

2 packages (2 tablespoons) dry yeast

⅓ cup nonfat powdered milk

½ cup shortening

⅓ cup sugar

1 teaspoon salt

2 eggs, beaten

¼ cup orange juice

2 tablespoons grated orange rind

5 to 6 cups flour, divided

Icing

2 tablespoons orange juice

1 teaspoon grated orange rind

1 cup confectioners' sugar

To make the rolls, pour the water into a large mixer bowl and sprinkle with the yeast. Add the milk, shortening, sugar, salt, eggs, orange juice, orange rind, and 3 cups of the flour. Blend on low, then beat on medium for 3 minutes. Add enough of the remaining flour to make a soft dough, either using the mixer's bread hook or stirring it in by hand. Turn the dough out onto a lightly floured surface and knead until smooth and elastic. Place in a greased bowl. Cover and let rise in a warm place until doubled in bulk, about 1½ hours.

Punch the dough down. Roll out to a ½-inch-thick rectangle that measures about 12x10 inches. Cut crosswise into ½-inch strips. Tie each strip into a knot and arrange on greased baking sheets. Cover and let rise until doubled in bulk, about 30 to 40 minutes.

Preheat the oven to 400°F. Bake for 8 to 10 minutes, or until golden brown. Cool on wire racks.

To make the icing, combine all the ingredients until well blended. Brush over the tops of the rolls.

Marjorie Johnson, Robbinsdale, Minnesota
Minnesota State Fair, St. Paul, Minnesota

Coffeecake Muffins

1 dozen muffins

These tasty muffins live up to their name. You'll find they are a winner with kids because of their sweet flavor.

Batter

- 1½ cups flour
- ½ cup sugar
- 2 teaspoons baking powder
- ½ teaspoon salt
- ½ cup vegetable oil
- 1 egg, slightly beaten
- ⅓ cup milk
- 1 teaspoon almond extract

Topping

- ¼ cup firmly packed brown sugar
- ¼ cup walnuts, chopped
- ¼ cup dried cherries, chopped
- 3 tablespoons flour
- 1 tablespoon butter or margarine, melted

Icing

- ½ cup confectioners' sugar
- 1 tablespoon milk
- 1 teaspoon almond extract

Preheat the oven to 350°F. Grease 12 muffin cups.

To make the batter, combine the flour, sugar, baking powder, and salt in a large bowl; mix well. In another bowl, combine the oil, egg, milk, and almond extract. Add to the flour mixture, stirring just until moistened.

To make the topping, combine the brown sugar, walnuts, cherries, and flour in a small bowl. Stir in the melted butter. Mix until crumbly.

Distribute half of the batter among the muffin cups. Sprinkle with half of the topping. Add the remaining batter and topping. Bake for 15 to 20 minutes, or until a toothpick inserted in the center comes out clean. Remove from the pan and cool on wire racks.

To make the icing, combine all the ingredients, mixing until smooth. Drizzle over the warm muffins. Serve warm or at room temperature.

Anne Smith, Traverse City, Michigan
National Cherry Festival, Traverse City, Michigan

Apricot Tea Ring

2 coffeecakes

Dough

- ½ cup milk
- ½ cup water
- ⅓ cup butter or margarine
- 4 cups flour, divided
- ⅓ cup sugar
- 1 teaspoon salt
- 2 packages (2 tablespoons) dry yeast
- 2 eggs
- 1 teaspoon grated orange rind
- ⅛ teaspoon ground mace

Filling

- 1¼ cups dried apricots, chopped
- ¼ cup water
- ¼ cup sugar
- ¼ teaspoon ground cinnamon
- ⅛ teaspoon salt
- 1 teaspoon grated lemon rind
- 1 tablespoon lemon juice

Glaze

- 1 cup confectioners' sugar
- 1 tablespoon milk or water
- ½ teaspoon butter, melted and cooled
- ½ teaspoon vanilla extract

Toasted sliced almonds

To make the dough, heat the milk, water, and butter to 120° to 130°F. In a large bowl, combine 2 cups of the flour, sugar, salt, and yeast. Add the hot liquid and beat for 3 minutes. Add the eggs, orange rind, and mace; beat well. Stir in the remaining 2 cups flour to make a soft dough. Turn out onto a lightly floured surface and knead until smooth, 3 to 5 minutes. Place in a greased bowl, cover, and let rise until doubled in bulk, about 1 hour.

Meanwhile, make the filling. Combine all the ingredients in a saucepan. Cook over medium heat, stirring constantly, until thickened, about 10 minutes. Cool.

Punch the dough down. Divide into 2 parts. Cover and let rest for 15 minutes. Roll each part out into a 22x7-inch rectangle. Spread each rectangle with about ⅔ cup filling. Starting with the long side, roll up jelly roll–style. Place in a ring shape on a greased baking sheet. At ½-inch intervals, make slashes down through the dough to within 1 inch of the pan. Cover and let rise until doubled in bulk, about 45 minutes.

For more recipes and kitchen tips, go to Almanac.com/food.

Preheat the oven to 375°F. Bake for 25 to 30 minutes, or until golden brown.

Meanwhile, make the glaze. Combine all the ingredients until creamy and spread on the coffeecake while it is still slightly warm. Sprinkle with the almonds.

Elaine Janas, Columbia Heights, Minnesota
Minnesota State Fair, St. Paul, Minnesota

★ ★ ★ ★ ★

FREEZING BAKED COFFEECAKES

I f you don't want to serve both these coffeecakes on the same day, it is easy to freeze one for later use. Wrap the unglazed coffeecake in aluminum foil and put it in a plastic bag, then freeze it. To thaw the coffeecake, remove it from the freezer and let it sit on the counter the night before you wish to serve it. Place it in a 200°F oven for 30 minutes, still wrapped in aluminum foil. Glaze and serve.

Bavarian Coffeecake

8 to 10 servings

This coffeecake both looks and tastes wonderful. For fruit lovers, the filling can accommodate another apple.

Dough

- 1 cup (2 sticks) butter, softened
- ¾ cup sugar
- 2 tablespoons sour cream
- 2 eggs, beaten
- 1 teaspoon vanilla extract
- 2¾ cups flour
- 2 teaspoons baking powder

Filling

- 2½ cups peeled, cored, and sliced baking apples
- 1 teaspoon ground cinnamon
- ½ cup golden raisins

- 2 tablespoons sugar

Preheat the oven to 350°F.

To make the dough, cream the butter and sugar. Mix in the sour cream, eggs, and vanilla. Add the flour and baking powder. (The dough will be soft and pliable.) Divide in half. Pat out one half to fit the bottom and sides of a greased 10-inch springform pan. Form an edge all around and puncture the bottom with a fork in a few places.

To make the filling, place the apples in concentric circles on the dough. Sprinkle with the cinnamon and raisins.

Pat out the remaining dough and cut into 1-inch-wide strips. Weave into a lattice over the apples. Sprinkle with the sugar and bake for about 1 hour, or until the apples are tender and the cake is golden brown. Serve warm.

Karin Gaysek, Kitchener, Ontario
The Old Farmer's Almanac *Recipe Contest, Dublin, New Hampshire*

Sour Cream Coffeecake #2

8 servings

Batter

- ¾ teaspoon baking soda
- 1 cup sour cream
- ¼ cup (½ stick) butter
- 1 cup sugar
- 1 large egg
- 1½ cups all-purpose flour
- 1½ teaspoons baking powder

Cinnamon-Nut Mixture

- 2 tablespoons sugar
- 1 teaspoon cinnamon
- ½ cup chopped nuts

Preheat the oven to 350°F. Butter and flour an 8x8-inch cake pan. In a small bowl, stir the baking soda into the sour cream and let stand for 5 to 10 minutes. (The sour cream will increase slightly in volume.) While the mixture is resting, stir together the cinnamon-nut mixture and set aside. In a large mixing bowl, cream the butter for 2 minutes with an electric mixer, then gradually add the sugar. Add the egg and beat until thoroughly combined. Add the sour-cream mixture, then beat in the flour and baking powder. Beat at medium speed for 2 minutes.

Spoon half the batter into the prepared pan. Sprinkle with the cinnamon-nut mixture. Smooth the remaining batter into the pan. Bake for 30 to 40 minutes, or until a toothpick inserted into the center comes out clean. Let stand for 10 minutes before removing from pan. Serve lukewarm or cold.

PAN SIZE SUBSTITUTIONS

★ ★ ★ ★ ★

I*n the midst of cooking but don't have the right pan? You can substitute one size for another, keeping in mind that when you change the pan size, you must sometimes change the cooking time. For example, if a recipe calls for using an 8-inch round cake pan and baking for 25 minutes, and you substitute a 9-inch pan, the cake may bake in only 20 minutes, since the batter forms a thinner layer in the larger pan. (Use a toothpick inserted into the center of the cake to test for doneness. If it comes out clean, the cake has finished baking.) Also, specialty pans such as tube and Bundt pans distribute heat differently; you may not get the same results if you substitute a regular cake pan for a specialty one, even if the volume is the same.*

PAN SIZE	VOLUME	SUBSTITUTE
9-inch pie pan	4 cups	8-inch round cake pan
8x4x2½-inch loaf pan	6 cups	Three 5x2-inch loaf pans Two 3x1¼-inch muffin tins 12x8x2-inch cake pan
9x5x3-inch loaf pan	8 cups	8-inch square cake pan 9-inch round cake pan
15x10x1-inch jelly-roll pan	10 cups	9-inch square cake pan Two 8-inch round cake pans 8x3-inch springform pan
10x3-inch Bundt pan	12 cups	Two 8x4x2½-inch loaf pans 9x3-inch angel food cake pan 9x3-inch springform pan
13x9x2-inch cake pan	14–15 cups	Two 9-inch round cake pans

Chapter 4

Frosted Cakes

Hungarian Nut Torte

8 to 10 servings

This heirloom recipe combines an Old World torte with an American-style frosting. For a more traditional presentation, try substituting a chocolate glaze such as the one for Swiss Chocolate Cake on page 72.

Torte

- 6 eggs, separated
- ⅞ cup sugar
- 2 tablespoons rum
- ½ cup fine unsalted cracker crumbs (about 12 crackers)
- ¼ cup grated unsweetened chocolate (about 1 ounce)
- ¾ cup walnuts, chopped
- ½ teaspoon baking powder
- ¼ teaspoon salt
- ½ teaspoon ground cinnamon
- ¼ teaspoon ground cloves
- ¼ teaspoon ground nutmeg

Frosting

- ⅓ cup butter, softened
- 3 cups confectioners' sugar, sifted
- 1 teaspoon vanilla extract
- 2 to 3 tablespoons milk or cream

- ½ cup walnuts, chopped
- ½ cup whipping cream, whipped

To make the torte, preheat the oven to 325°F. Beat the egg yolks until light. Add the sugar gradually and beat until well blended. Stir in the rum. In another bowl, combine the crumbs, chocolate, walnuts, baking powder, salt, cinnamon, cloves, and nutmeg. Add to the egg mixture and blend thoroughly. With clean beaters, beat the egg whites until stiff and fold into the batter. Pour into an ungreased 9-inch springform pan and bake for 35 to 45 minutes, or until a toothpick inserted in the center comes out clean. Cool in the pan on a wire rack for about 45 minutes. Remove the sides of the pan.

To make the frosting, beat the butter, confectioners' sugar, vanilla, and enough milk or cream to achieve a spreading consistency. Spread on the sides of the torte.

Pat the walnuts on the frosting. Pipe the whipped cream around the top edge.

Helen L. Harter, Rome, New York
The Old Farmer's Almanac *Recipe Contest, Dublin, New Hampshire*

Cream Cheese Cake

10 to 12 servings

A moist cake with a richer flavor than the average white cake.

Cake

- ½ cup (1 stick) butter, softened
- 1 package (8 ounces) cream cheese, softened
- 1¼ cups sugar
- 2 eggs
- 1 teaspoon vanilla extract
- ½ cup milk
- 2 cups flour
- 2 teaspoons baking powder
- ½ teaspoon baking soda
- ½ teaspoon salt

Filling

- 2 packages (8 ounces each) cream cheese, softened
- ½ cup fruit preserves

Frosting

- 2 packages (8 ounces each) cream cheese, softened
- 1 cup confectioners' sugar
- 1 teaspoon vanilla extract

To make the cake, preheat the oven to 350°F. Grease and flour two 9-inch round cake pans. Cream the butter and cream cheese until fluffy and light. Add all the remaining ingredients. Mix on low for 30 seconds. Beat on medium for 3 minutes, scraping the bowl occasionally. Pour into the prepared pans and bake for 30 to 35 minutes, or until a toothpick inserted in the center comes out clean. Cool in the pans on wire racks for 5 minutes. Remove from the pans and cool completely on racks.

To make the filling, blend the cream cheese and preserves until smooth. Spread thickly on top of one layer and place the other layer on it.

To make the frosting, blend all the ingredients until smooth. Frost the sides and top of the cake. Keep refrigerated until serving time.

Robin Laabs, Milwaukee, Wisconsin
Wisconsin State Fair, West Allis, Wisconsin

BLUE RIBBON TIP

★ ★ ★ ★ ★

ALL FLOUR IS NOT CREATED EQUAL

All-purpose flour sounds like the sort of thing that ought to be pretty much the same anywhere. However, this turns out not to be true. All-purpose flour can be made from either hard wheat or a mixture of hard and soft wheats. This difference can dramatically affect the level of gluten in the finished product. For example, all-purpose flour in the North tends to be made with more hard wheat, while all-purpose flour in the South and West tends to have more soft wheat in it.

Because "hardness" is a measure of protein content, not texture, all-purpose flour made from hard wheat has a higher protein content than flour made from a blend of wheats or flour made from soft wheat such as cake flour (see page 70). Hard-wheat flours have less starch and form strong gluten, giving structure to yeast breads. However, in making cakes, this means that the more you beat the batter, the more you develop the gluten, which can result in a tougher texture. Denser cakes, such as pound cakes, and cakes with added seeds or nuts, turn out well with all-purpose flour.

Moist Chocolate Cake with Cocoa Butter Frosting

10 to 12 servings

Cake

- 2 cups flour
- 1 teaspoon salt
- 1 teaspoon baking powder
- 2 teaspoons baking soda
- ¾ cup unsweetened cocoa
- 2 cups sugar
- 1 cup vegetable oil
- 1 cup hot coffee
- 1 cup milk
- 2 eggs
- 1 teaspoon vanilla extract

Frosting

- ⅓ cup butter, softened
- ⅓ cup unsweetened cocoa
- 2 cups confectioners' sugar
- 1½ teaspoons vanilla extract
- 2 tablespoons milk (approximately)

To make the cake, preheat the oven to 325°F. Grease and flour two 9-inch round cake pans. In a mixer bowl, sift together the flour, salt, baking powder, baking soda, cocoa, and sugar. Add the oil, coffee, and milk. Beat for 2 minutes. Add the eggs and vanilla and beat for 2 minutes more. (The batter will be thin.) Pour into the prepared pans and bake for 25 to 35 minutes, or until a toothpick inserted in the center comes out clean. Cool in the pans on wire racks for 10 minutes. Remove from the pans and cool completely on racks before frosting.

To make the frosting, use an electric mixer to cream the butter and cocoa. Beat in the confectioners' sugar. Beat in the vanilla and enough milk to make the frosting of spreading consistency. Spread frosting on top of one cake and place the other cake on it. Frost the sides and top of the cake.

Carolyn Moreton, Flemington, New Jersey
Hunterdon County 4-H and Agricultural Fair, Flemington, New Jersey

Peanut Butter Chocolate Chip Cupcakes

1 dozen large or 2 dozen small cupcakes

These delicious cupcakes are a guaranteed kid pleaser.

Cupcakes

- ½ cup creamy peanut butter
- ½ cup (1 stick) butter, softened
- 1½ cups brown sugar
- 2 eggs
- 1 teaspoon vanilla extract
- 2 cups flour
- ½ teaspoon salt
- 1½ teaspoons baking powder
- ¾ cup milk
- ½ cup semisweet chocolate chips

Frosting

- ⅓ cup butter, softened
- ⅓ cup unsweetened cocoa
- 2 cups confectioners' sugar
- 1½ teaspoons vanilla extract
- 2 tablespoons milk

To make the cupcakes, preheat the oven to 375°F. Line muffin cups with paper liners. Cream the peanut butter, butter, and brown sugar until fluffy. Beat in the eggs and vanilla. Sift together the flour, salt, and baking powder. Add to the batter alternately with the milk. Stir in the chocolate chips. Fill the muffin cups one-half to three-quarters full. Bake for 20 minutes, or until a toothpick inserted in the center comes out clean. Cool completely.

To make the frosting, cream the butter until fluffy. Beat in the cocoa.

Beat in the confectioners' sugar. Add the vanilla and milk and beat to spreading consistency. Frost the cupcakes.

Kate Thomas, Fitzwilliam, New Hampshire
Shelburne Grange Fair, Shelburne, Massachusetts

Date and Walnut Cake

12 servings

Cake

- 1 cup dates, chopped
- 1 teaspoon baking soda
- 1 cup boiling water
- 1 tablespoon butter
- 1 cup sugar
- 1 egg
- 1⅓ cups flour
- ½ cup walnuts, chopped

Frosting

- 1 package (8 ounces) cream cheese, softened
- 1 box (1 pound) confectioners' sugar

Candied cherries (optional)
Walnut halves (optional)

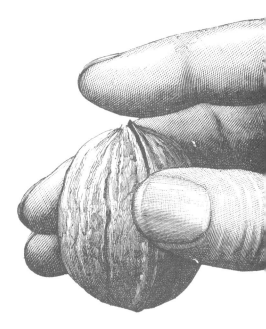

To make the cake, preheat the oven to 350°F. Grease a 9-inch round cake pan or an 8½x4½-inch loaf pan. Place the dates and baking soda in a small bowl and pour the boiling water over them. Let stand for 10 minutes. Cream the butter and sugar. Add the date mixture and egg and beat well. Add the flour and chopped walnuts and pour into the prepared pan. Bake the round layer for 30 to 40 minutes or the loaf for 50 to 60 minutes, or until a toothpick inserted in the center comes out clean. Let cool in the pan for 10 minutes. Remove from the pan and cool on a wire rack.

To make the frosting, beat the cream cheese, adding the confectioners' sugar gradually. Beat to spreading consistency. Spread on the thoroughly cooled cake. Garnish with candied cherries and walnut halves if desired.

Nancy McDowell, Desert Center, California
National Date Festival, Indio, California

Chocolate Torte with Vanilla Sauce and Raspberries

8 to 12 servings

This dense and super-chocolaty torte should satisfy the most confirmed chocolate maniac.

Torte

- 9 squares (9 ounces) semisweet chocolate, coarsely chopped
- 3 tablespoons raspberry liqueur
- 2 tablespoons milk
- 14 tablespoons unsalted butter, cut into tablespoon-size pieces
- 1 cup sugar, divided
- 13 tablespoons flour, sifted
- 5 eggs, separated
- Pinch of salt
- Pinch of cream of tartar

Glaze

- 6 tablespoons whipping cream
- 2 tablespoons raspberry liqueur
- 8 squares (8 ounces) semisweet chocolate, coarsely chopped

Vanilla Sauce

- 2 cups heavy cream
- 2 teaspoons vanilla extract
- 2 eggs
- ½ cup sugar

- 2 cups fresh raspberries

To make the torte, preheat the oven to 350°F. Butter a 9-inch springform pan or round cake pan with 2-inch sides. Line the bottom with wax paper. Butter the paper and dust with flour. Melt the chocolate with the liqueur and milk in the top of a double boiler. Add the butter one piece at a time, whisking until melted. Remove from the heat and whisk in ¾ cup of the sugar, flour, and egg yolks. Beat the egg whites with the salt and cream of tartar until soft peaks form. Add the remaining ¼ cup sugar 1 tablespoon at a time and beat until stiff but not dry. Whisk the chocolate mixture lightly, then fold in one-fourth of the egg whites. Fold the chocolate mixture back into the remaining whites. Pour into the prepared pan. Bake for about 1¼ hours, or until the center feels firm. (The top will crack.) Cool in the pan on a wire rack for 15 minutes. Turn out onto the rack, remove the wax paper, and turn over onto another rack. Cool completely.

To make the glaze, scald the cream with the liqueur in a heavy saucepan. Remove from the heat. Add the chocolate a little at a time, stirring until melted and heating slightly if necessary. Cool until thick enough to spread.

For more recipes and kitchen tips, go to Almanac.com/food.

To make the vanilla sauce, combine the cream and vanilla in a saucepan. Heat just until boiling. Remove from the heat. In a large bowl, beat the eggs and sugar together. Add the hot cream in a slow stream, whisking steadily. Return the mixture to the saucepan. Cook over moderate heat, stirring with a wooden spoon, until thickened. Pour into a stainless steel bowl and set in a larger bowl of ice water. When cold, cover and refrigerate.

Invert the cake, flat side up, onto a platter. Spread the glaze evenly over the sides and top. Refrigerate until the glaze is firm. Serve at room temperature with the vanilla sauce and fresh raspberries.

Marilyn Neumayer, Manchester, Connecticut
Great New England Food Festival, Boston, Massachusetts

★ ★ ★ ★ ★

SERVING A PRETTY CAKE

To keep the bottom of a frosted or glazed cake neat, place four strips of wax paper around and just under the bottom of the cake before frosting or glazing. Wait for the frosting or glaze to set completely, slide a knife carefully around the bottom of the cake, and gently pull out the wax paper. The edge of the cake and the platter will be nice and neat.

CAKE FLOUR:
THE BAKER'S SECRET INGREDIENT

Cake flour is much finer than all-purpose flour, but this is not just because it is more finely milled. Cake flour is always made from soft wheat. Compared to hard wheat, soft wheat contains a little less of the two proteins that, when combined with water, form gluten. This means that cake flour is less likely to form elastic sheets of gluten that will interfere with the fast leavening action of baking powder or soda. Cake flour also has been chlorinated to permit a better distribution of the bubbles formed by the baking powder and soda, yielding a moist, velvety texture. Professional bakers almost always use cake flour to get that distinctive light texture we associate with bakery cakes.

If you substitute all-purpose flour for cake flour, use 2 tablespoons less flour per cup. Or use 2 tablespoons less all-purpose flour per cup of cake flour and add 2 tablespoons of cornstarch, which will enhance the sweetness of the cake.

Ultimately, it's a matter of taste: Choose cake flour if you prefer a high volume and airy texture. Choose an unbleached, high-quality, all-purpose flour for a heady, moist cake that will still taste good.

Forest Chiffon Cake

12 servings

Cake

2¼ cups cake flour
¾ cup granulated sugar
¾ cup firmly packed brown sugar
3 teaspoons baking powder
1 teaspoon salt
¾ cup cold water
½ cup vegetable oil
2 teaspoons maple flavoring
2 teaspoons black walnut extract
5 egg yolks
1 cup egg whites (about 8 eggs)
½ teaspoon cream of tartar
1 cup walnuts, finely chopped

Frosting

1 cup (2 sticks) butter or margarine, softened
3 cups confectioners' sugar
3 tablespoons firmly packed brown sugar
2 tablespoons maple syrup
2 teaspoons black walnut extract
1 to 2 tablespoons milk (optional)

¼ cup walnuts, chopped (optional)

To make the cake, preheat the oven to 325°F. Combine the flour, granulated sugar, brown sugar, baking powder, and salt in a large bowl. Using a wooden spoon, beat in the water, oil, maple flavoring, black walnut extract, and egg yolks until smooth. In another large bowl, beat the egg whites and cream of tartar until stiff peaks form. Gradually pour the batter over the egg whites, folding them in with a rubber spatula until just blended. Fold in the walnuts. Pour into an ungreased 10-inch tube pan. Bake for 55 minutes. Increase the oven temperature to 350°F and bake for 10 to 15 minutes more, or until the top springs back when lightly touched. Immediately turn the cake upside down onto a glass bottle or metal funnel. Let hang for about 2 hours, or until the cake is completely cool. Remove from the pan.

To make the frosting, beat the butter for 30 seconds. Add the confectioners' sugar and beat on low until fluffy. Add the brown sugar, maple syrup, and black walnut extract. Beat on high until smooth, creamy, and thick enough to spread, adding enough milk (if necessary) to achieve a spreading consistency. Frost the cake. Sprinkle with walnuts if desired.

Lilly R. Koski, Pueblo, Colorado
Colorado State Fair, Pueblo, Colorado

Swiss Chocolate Cake

12 servings

This is a true, flourless torte. Your guests will feel as though they have dropped into a coffee shop in old Europe when they taste this scrumptious, light confection.

Cake

- 2 cups ground toasted hazelnuts
- 3 teaspoons baking powder
- 4 squares (4 ounces) semisweet chocolate
- ½ cup (1 stick) butter or margarine
- 1 cup sugar
- 6 eggs, separated
- 1 teaspoon vanilla extract

Glaze

- 4 squares (4 ounces) semisweet chocolate
- ¼ cup water
- 2 tablespoons butter or margarine
- ¼ cup confectioners' sugar, sifted

- ½ cup toasted hazelnuts, chopped (optional)

To make the cake, preheat the oven to 375°F. Trace the bottom of an 8- or 9-inch springform pan on wax paper and cut out the circle. Grease the pan, place the wax paper in the pan, and grease the paper. Combine the hazelnuts and baking powder in a small bowl. Melt the chocolate in the top of a double boiler. Cool. Cream the butter and sugar until fluffy. Beat in the egg yolks one at a time. Add the vanilla and melted chocolate and beat well. Stir in the hazelnut mixture.

With clean beaters, beat the egg whites until stiff but not dry. Stir about one-third of the egg whites into the hazelnut mixture. Fold in the remaining egg whites as gently as possible. Pour the batter into the prepared pan. Bake for 1 hour, or until a toothpick inserted in the center comes out clean. (The cake will fall in the center.) Cool in the pan on a wire rack. Remove from the pan and discard the wax paper.

To make the glaze, melt the chocolate with the water in the top of a double boiler. Stir in the butter and confectioners' sugar until smooth and blended. Spread a thin layer on the sides of the thoroughly cooled cake. Spread the remaining glaze on top. Garnish the sides with chopped hazelnuts if desired.

Nicole Primeau, Springfield, Oregon
Springfield Filbert Festival, Springfield, Oregon

★ ★ ★ ★ ★

TOASTING & GRINDING NUTS

T o toast hazelnuts, also called filberts, place the whole nuts in a baking pan. Bake in a 350°F oven for 10 to 15 minutes. Roll the hot nuts in a wet towel to remove as many of the husks as possible.

To get the right texture for ground nuts, it is necessary to use the kind of grater commonly used for Parmesan cheese. A food processor will pulverize the nuts into small enough pieces, but it also will release too much of the oil. Hand-chopping will not get the pieces small enough or even enough. One cup of toasted hazelnuts should yield 2 cups of ground nuts.

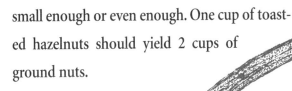

Nany's Caramel Peanut Butter Cake

10 to 16 servings

Terri Spitler created this cake in honor of her grandmother, Mildred Snell. It is an adaptation of a cake her grandmother made often. This one is a real showstopper because it contains five layers! (If you don't have five 8-inch pans, plan to bake the layers in batches.)

Cake

- 1 cup shortening
- 2½ cups sugar
- 6 eggs
- 3 cups flour, sifted
- 1 teaspoon baking powder
- ½ teaspoon salt
- 1 cup buttermilk
- 1 teaspoon vanilla extract

Filling

- 1 package (8 ounces) cream cheese, softened
- ¼ cup (½ stick) butter or margarine
- 1 box (1 pound) confectioners' sugar
- ½ cup creamy peanut butter
- ½ teaspoon vanilla extract

Frosting

- ½ cup (1 stick) butter or margarine
- 1½ cups lightly packed brown sugar
- ¼ cup light corn syrup
- 1 box (1 pound) confectioners' sugar
- ⅓ cup evaporated milk
- 1 teaspoon vanilla extract
- 1 cup extra-crunchy peanut butter

To make the cake, preheat the oven to 400°F. Grease five 8-inch round cake pans. Cut five circles out of waxed paper to line the pans. Grease the paper and flour the pans and paper. Beat the shortening until fluffy. Gradually add the sugar. When well mixed, add the eggs one at a time, mixing well after each addition. Sift together the flour, baking powder, and salt. Add to the egg mixture 1 cup at a time, alternating with the buttermilk. Add the vanilla and mix only until combined. Pour into the prepared pans, using a heaping ½ cup for each layer. Spread to the edges of the pans and smooth. Bake for about 20 minutes, or until a toothpick inserted in the center comes out clean. Remove from the pans to wire racks. Remove the wax paper and cool completely.

To make the filling, cream the cream cheese and butter until well blended. Add the confectioners' sugar and continue beating until creamy. Add the peanut butter and vanilla. Spread on one cake layer. Place another layer on top and spread with filling. Continue stacking and spreading filling between the layers.

To make the frosting, melt the butter with the brown sugar and corn syrup in a saucepan. Bring to a boil. Remove from the heat, add the confectioners' sugar, evaporated milk, vanilla, and peanut butter. Beat until creamy. Spread on the top and sides of the cake.

Terri Spitler, Dothan, Alabama
National Peanut Festival, Dothan, Alabama

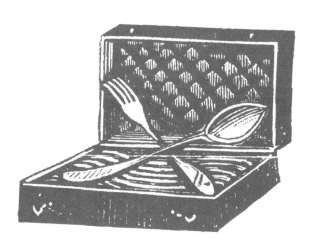

Linzertorte Cake

12 to 16 servings

This cake makes a very dramatic and impressive finale for any special dinner, looking as though it came straight out of a fancy European bakery. Your friends will surely award it a blue ribbon. Well worth the effort.

Cake

- 1 cup toasted hazelnuts
- 2 cups flour
- 1 tablespoon baking powder
- 1½ teaspoons Chinese five-spice powder
- ½ teaspoon ground nutmeg
- ½ teaspoon salt
- ¾ cup (1½ sticks) unsalted butter, softened
- 1½ cups sugar
- 3 egg yolks
- 2 teaspoons vanilla extract
- 1 teaspoon almond extract
- 1¼ cups whole milk
- 5 egg whites, at room temperature

Frosting

- 6 ounces good-quality white chocolate
- 3 packages (8 ounces each) cream cheese, softened
- 9 tablespoons unsalted butter, softened
- 1½ cups confectioners' sugar
- 2¼ teaspoons vanilla extract
- ½ teaspoon almond extract

- 1 cup raspberry preserves, stirred to soften, divided
- 1½ cups toasted hazelnuts, finely chopped

To make the cake, preheat the oven to 350°F. Butter a 15x10-inch jellyroll pan. Line the pan with parchment or wax paper and grease the paper. Flour the pan and paper. Finely grind the nuts with the flour in a blender. (Be sure not to overprocess. For more information on working with nuts, see page 73.) Transfer to a medium bowl. Mix in the baking powder, five-spice powder, nutmeg, and salt. Using an electric mixer, beat the butter and sugar until well blended. Beat in the egg yolks, vanilla, and almond extract. On low speed, beat in the dry ingredients alternately with the milk, beating just until combined. The batter will be thick.

Using a clean bowl and beaters, beat the egg whites until stiff peaks form. Fold one-third of the whites into the batter. Fold in the remaining whites carefully. Spread the batter in the prepared pan. Bake until a toothpick inserted in the center comes out clean, about 25 minutes. Cool in the pan on a wire rack for 20 minutes. Remove from the pan onto a layer of wax paper or aluminum foil on a wire rack. Carefully peel off

For more recipes and kitchen tips, go to Almanac.com/food.

the parchment or wax paper on the bottom. Cool completely.

To make the frosting, melt the white chocolate in the top of a double boiler. Cool to barely lukewarm. Using an electric mixer, beat the cream cheese and butter in a large bowl. Beat in the white chocolate, then the confectioners' sugar, vanilla, and almond extract. Work quickly to prevent the chocolate from setting.

Using a serrated knife, carefully cut the cake crosswise into three 10x5-inch rectangles. Carefully place one rectangle on a platter. Spread ¾ cup frosting over the cake. Drizzle with ¼ cup of the raspberry preserves. Top with a second cake layer and spread with ¾ cup frosting and drizzle with ¼ cup preserves. Top with a third cake layer. Place 1¼ cups frosting in a pastry bag fitted with a ¼-inch plain or star tip. Cover the sides and top of the cake with the remaining frosting. Spread the remaining ½ cup preserves over the top, covering it evenly. Pipe frosting in a lattice pattern on top of the cake (7 diagonal lines in each direction). Gently press the chopped hazelnuts onto the sides. Pipe a line of frosting around the top edge where the frosting and nuts meet. Store in the refrigerator. Let stand for at least 2 hours at room temperature before serving.

Theresa S. Martin, Essex Junction, Vermont
Champlain Valley Fair and Exposition,
  Essex Junction, Vermont

BLUE RIBBON TIP

★ ★ ★ ★

IS WHITE CHOCOLATE REALLY CHOCOLATE?

Some people say that white chocolate is not real chocolate because it contains no cocoa solids. Good-quality white chocolate, however, does contain cocoa butter and is truly delicious. When melted, it sets faster than dark chocolate, so you have to work fast. At room temperature, white chocolate is a little softer than dark. Note that because it contains milk solids, its shelf life is much shorter than that of dark chocolate.

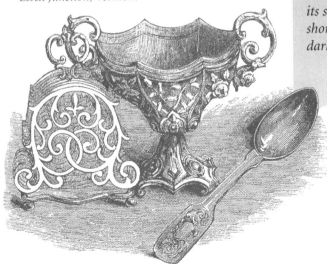

White Cake with Coconut and Whipped Cream

12 servings

The fresh coconut in this recipe is so different and refreshing that it makes this cake a memorable one.

Cake

- 3 cups cake flour
- 1½ teaspoons baking powder
- ½ teaspoon baking soda
- 1 teaspoon salt
- ⅓ cup butter
- ⅓ cup shortening
- 1¾ cups sugar
- ½ teaspoon almond extract
- ½ teaspoon lemon extract
- 1 teaspoon vanilla extract
- 4 egg whites
- 1⅓ cups buttermilk

Filling

- 1 cup sour cream
- 1 cup confectioners' sugar
- 3 cups frozen or freshly grated coconut (about 1 coconut)

Whipped Cream

- 2 cups whipping cream, well chilled
- 5 tablespoons confectioners' sugar, sifted
- 1 teaspoon vanilla extract

Sweetened coconut (optional)
Maraschino cherry (optional)

To make the cake, preheat the oven to 375°F. Grease and flour two 9-inch round cake pans. Sift together the flour, baking powder, baking soda, and salt. In a large bowl, cream the butter and shortening. Add the sugar, creaming thoroughly. Stir in the almond, lemon, and vanilla extracts. Add half the egg whites and beat vigorously until fluffy. Add the remaining egg whites and beat again. Add the dry ingredients and buttermilk alternately, stirring well. Pour into the prepared pans and bake for 23 to 25 minutes, or until a toothpick inserted in the center comes out clean. Cool in the pans on wire racks for 5 minutes. When barely cool, remove from the pans and split the layers in half with a thread or bread knife.

To make the filling, combine all the ingredients in a large bowl. Whisk until fluffy.

To make the whipped cream, combine all the ingredients in a chilled bowl and whip with a chilled beater until stiff peaks form.

Place one-quarter of the whipped cream on top of the first split layer, spreading evenly to a ½-inch thickness. Spoon one-quarter of the filling on top of the cream and spread it to the edges of the cake. Repeat for each split layer, stacking the layers as you go. After the cream and filling are spread on top of the cake, sprinkle with coconut and garnish with a maraschino cherry if desired. Keep cake chilled until serving time.

Annie Davis, Watauga, Tennessee
Appalachian Fair, Gray, Tennessee

★ ★ ★ ★ ★

CRACKING THE COCONUT

Fresh coconut adds a whole different flavor to your baking. To choose a good coconut, make sure that you can hear the liquid inside when you shake it. To open it, make two holes with a screwdriver and hammer and pour the liquid out. Using a hammer or the back side of a cleaver or heavy knife, hit the coconut repeatedly around its equator until it cracks open. Break the coconut into smaller pieces with a hammer. Remove the shell by slipping a knife between it and the meat and prying the shell off. Use a vegetable peeler to scrape off the brown skin. Cut the coconut into 1-inch pieces and grate by chopping in a food processor or blender. Frozen coconut is available in many Mexican and Latin American specialty stores. It defrosts quickly and is very easy to use.

Black Walnut Layer Cake

12 servings

This is a scrumptious and very memorable cake featuring the distinctive flavor of the American black walnut.

Cake

- 2 cups flour
- 1 teaspoon baking soda
- ¼ teaspoon salt
- ½ cup (1 stick) butter or margarine
- ½ cup shortening
- 2 cups sugar
- 5 eggs, separated
- 1 teaspoon vanilla extract
- 1 cup buttermilk
- 1½ cups chopped black walnuts
- 1 cup sweetened coconut
- ½ teaspoon cream of tartar

Frosting

- ½ cup (1 stick) butter or margarine
- 1 package (8 ounces) cream cheese
- 1 teaspoon vanilla extract
- 3½ cups confectioners' sugar

- ½ cup sweetened coconut
- ½ cup chopped black walnuts

To make the cake, preheat the oven to 350°F. Generously grease and flour three 9-inch round cake pans. In a medium bowl, sift together the flour, baking soda, and salt. In a large bowl, combine the butter, shortening, and sugar. Beat until smooth and well blended. Add the egg yolks and vanilla and beat well. Add the flour mixture gradually, alternating with the buttermilk, and beat until the batter is smooth. Stir in the walnuts and coconut.

Using clean beaters and a medium bowl, beat the egg whites and cream of tartar until stiff but moist peaks form. Gently fold into the batter. Divide the batter evenly between the prepared pans. Bake for 30 minutes, or until a toothpick inserted in the center comes out clean. Cool in the pans on wire racks for 10 minutes. Remove from the pans and cool completely on racks.

To make the frosting, in a medium bowl cream the butter, cream cheese, and vanilla until well blended. Beat in the confectioners' sugar and continue beating until the mixture is smooth and of spreading consistency. Frost the top of one layer and place another layer on it. Frost the top of this layer and place the third layer on it. Frost the sides and top of the cake.

Sprinkle coconut on top and carefully sprinkle black walnuts in a ring around the outside edge of the cake.

Nancy Johnson, Clever, Missouri
Ozark Empire Fair, Springfield, Missouri

★ ★ ★ ★ ★

THE ELUSIVE BLACK WALNUT

Most of us are used to English walnuts. The native American species is called the American black walnut and has a rich, distinctive flavor. You'll have to search to find them (some health food and specialty food stores carry them), but this blue ribbon winner will show them off to their best advantage. One source of black walnuts is Hammons Pantry, 105 Hammons Dr., Stockton, MO 65785; 888-429-6887; www.black-walnuts.com. If you must, you may substitute English walnuts for American black walnuts.

Chocolate Coconut Cream Cake

10 to 12 servings

With this recipe, Renee Janas-Johnson has won the grand sweepstakes in the cake category at this fair, as well as the General Mills Softasilk Flour Contest and the Nestlé Choco-Bake Challenge.

Cake

- 2 cups cake flour
- 2 cups sugar
- 1 teaspoon baking soda
- 1 teaspoon salt
- ½ teaspoon baking powder
- ¾ cup water
- ¾ cup buttermilk
- ½ cup shortening
  (do not use butter)
- 2 eggs
- 1 teaspoon coconut extract
- 4 envelopes (1 ounce each) premelted unsweetened chocolate

Filling

- ¼ cup (½ stick) butter, softened
- ¼ cup shortening
- 1 cup marshmallow cream
- 1½ teaspoons coconut extract
- 1¼ cups confectioners' sugar, sifted

Frosting

- ½ cup milk
- ¼ cup (½ stick) butter
- 1 cup semisweet chocolate chips
- 1 teaspoon vanilla extract
- 2½ cups confectioners' sugar, sifted

Toasted coconut (optional)

To make the cake, preheat the oven to 350°F. Grease and flour two 9-inch round aluminum cake pans (do not use nonstick pans). To make the cake, place all the ingredients in a large mixer bowl. Blend for 30 seconds on low, scraping the bowl constantly. Beat for 3 minutes on high, scraping the bowl occasionally. Pour evenly into the prepared pans. Bake for 30 to 35 minutes, or until a toothpick inserted in the center comes out clean. (Do not overbake.) Cool in the pans on wire racks for 10 minutes. Remove from the pans and cool completely on racks.

To make the filling, cream the butter and shortening thoroughly. Add the marshmallow cream and coconut extract and beat well. Add the confectioners' sugar and beat until smooth. Spread half of the filling over one cake layer. Place the second cake layer on top and cover with the remaining filling.

To make the frosting, place the milk, butter, and chocolate chips in a saucepan over medium heat, stirring constantly until the chocolate and butter are melted. Remove from the heat and add the vanilla and confectioners' sugar. Mix until smooth. Frost the sides of the cake. Put the remaining frosting in a pastry bag fitted with a star tip and pipe around the top and bottom. If desired, sprinkle toasted coconut inside the piping on top.

Renee Janas-Johnson, Brooklyn Park, Minnesota
Minnesota State Fair, St. Paul, Minnesota

Pumpkin Cake

12 servings

Tammy Reiss is no stranger to blue ribbons, and this cake is a consistent winner. Our recipe tester rates it "absolutely delicious."

Cake

- 1½ cups vegetable oil
- 2 cups flour
- 2 cups sugar
- 1½ cups solid-pack pumpkin
- 4 eggs
- 2 teaspoons baking soda
- 3 teaspoons ground cinnamon
- 1 teaspoon vanilla extract

Frosting

- 1 package (8 ounces) cream cheese
- ¼ cup (½ stick) butter
- 2½ cups confectioners' sugar
- 2 teaspoons vanilla extract
- 1 cup nuts, chopped

To make the cake, preheat the oven to 350°F. Mix all the ingredients together until smooth. Pour into a greased 12-cup Bundt pan and bake for 1½ hours, or until a toothpick inserted in the cake comes out clean. Cool in the pan on a wire rack for 10 to 15 minutes. Remove from the pan.

To make the frosting, beat the cream cheese and butter. Beat in the confectioners' sugar and vanilla. Stir in the nuts and spread on the cake while it is still slightly warm.

Tammy Reiss, Moore, Oklahoma
Oklahoma State Fair, Oklahoma City, Oklahoma

The Best Carrot Cake Ever

About 24 servings

Cake

- 1¾ cups sugar
- ¾ cup vegetable oil
- 1 teaspoon vanilla extract
- 4 eggs
- 2 cups all-purpose flour
- ½ teaspoon ground nutmeg
- 1½ teaspoons cinnamon
- 2 teaspoons baking powder
- 1 teaspoon baking soda
- 2 cups lightly packed shredded carrots
- 1 can (8 ounces) pineapple tidbits, drained
- ¾ cup chopped walnuts

Cream Cheese Frosting

- 6 ounces (2 small packages) cream cheese, softened
- 6 tablespoons butter, softened
- 1 teaspoon minced orange peel
- 2 to 2¼ cups confectioners' sugar, sifted

Preheat the oven to 350°F. Grease and flour a 13x9-inch baking pan. In a mixing bowl, beat together the sugar, oil, and vanilla just until combined. At medium speed, beat in the eggs one at a time. Stir in the flour, nutmeg, cinnamon, baking powder, and baking soda. Add the carrots, pineapple, and nuts. Stir just until combined. Pour the batter into the prepared pan. Bake until a knife inserted into the center comes out clean, about 45 minutes. Remove from the oven, place onto a rack, and let cool.

For frosting: Combine all ingredients and beat until smooth. Adjust the amount of confectioners' sugar, depending on how stiff you like the icing to be.

Gingerbread Cake

12 to 14 servings

2 cups applesauce	½ teaspoon ground cloves
1 cup dark molasses	4 eggs
2 teaspoons baking soda	1⅓ cups sugar
3 cups sifted all-purpose flour	⅔ cup vegetable oil
½ teaspoon salt	
3 teaspoons powdered ginger	White Glaze (recipe below)
1½ teaspoons cinnamon	

Preheat the oven to 325°F. In a large saucepan, slowly bring the applesauce to a boil. Stir in the molasses and baking soda. (The mixture will foam up.) Set aside to cool. In a medium bowl, combine the flour, salt, and spices, and stir with a whisk to blend. In a large bowl, beat the eggs with an electric mixer for several minutes, until light. Gradually add the sugar and continue beating until thick. Gradually beat in the oil. With the mixer on low speed, alternately fold in the flour mixture and the applesauce mixture. Pour the batter into a well-greased 10-inch tube pan and bake for 1 hour and 15 minutes. Cool the cake in the pan for 15 minutes, then unmold and continue to cool on a rack. Decorate with White Glaze.

White Glaze

¼ cup (½ stick) butter
2 cups confectioners' sugar
3 tablespoons milk

Melt the butter in a small saucepan over low heat. Stir in the confectioners' sugar and milk and beat for several minutes, until smooth. (If the mixture seems too thin, let it cool slightly, to thicken.) Pour over the cooled cake, letting it run down the sides.

For more recipes and kitchen tips, go to Almanac.com/food.

Apple-Walnut Celebration Cake

12 to 16 servings

¾ cup (1½ sticks) butter
1½ cups sugar
2 eggs
1 cup plain yogurt
½ teaspoon grated nutmeg
2 cups flour
1 teaspoon baking powder
1 teaspoon baking soda

½ teaspoon salt
1 teaspoon cinnamon
2 large, tart apples, peeled and grated
¾ cup finely chopped walnuts

Cream Cheese Frosting (recipe below)

Preheat the oven to 350°F. Butter an 8-cup Bundt pan or tube pan, using melted butter and a brush. In a mixing bowl, cream the butter and sugar. Beat in eggs one at a time. Add yogurt and nutmeg and beat until smooth. In a separate bowl, mix dry ingredients with a fork and add to yogurt mixture, combining thoroughly but not beating. Stir in apples and nuts. Spoon batter into prepared pan and bake 50 minutes, or until done. Cool in pan for 10 minutes and unmold. Dust with confectioners' sugar or frost with Cream Cheese Frosting.

Cream Cheese Frosting

3 ounces cream cheese, softened
¼ cup (½ stick) butter, softened
1½ cups confectioners' sugar, sifted

Combine cream cheese and butter and beat until smooth. Add confectioners' sugar, beating at low speed until well blended.

The Best
Chocolate Birthday Cake

12 to 16 servings

3 ounces unsweetened baking chocolate
1⅓ cups strong, brewed coffee, divided
¾ cup (1½ sticks) butter
2¼ cups packed brown sugar
2 eggs
1 teaspoon vanilla extract
2 cups sifted flour
1 teaspoon baking soda
½ teaspoon salt

Dark Chocolate Frosting (recipe at right)

Preheat the oven to 350°F. Melt chocolate in ⅓ cup coffee over very low heat, stirring constantly. When melted, set aside to cool slightly. In a mixing bowl, cream butter and brown sugar. Add eggs one at a time and beat well. Add vanilla, blend in chocolate mixture, and beat well. Combine and fork-mix dry ingredients, and add alternately with 1 cup coffee, mixing just enough to combine, by hand or on lowest mixer speed.

Pour batter into two well-buttered 9-inch cake pans lined with buttered waxed paper. Bake for 30 minutes, or until a toothpick inserted into the center comes out clean. Do not remove cake too soon or it will fall. Cool 10 minutes in pan, then remove and cool on rack. (Layers are fragile; handle carefully.) Frost with Dark Chocolate Frosting.

Dark Chocolate Frosting

Frosts 2 layers

3 ounces unsweetened chocolate
¼ cup (½ stick) butter, at room temperature
4 cups sifted confectioners' sugar
¼ teaspoon salt
⅓ to ½ cup strong, brewed coffee
1 teaspoon vanilla extract

Melt chocolate in a double boiler. Add butter and stir until blended. Pour into a mixing bowl. Beat in confectioners' sugar and salt alternately with a few drops of coffee at a time, until frosting reaches the proper consistency. Beat in vanilla.

Zucchini-Yogurt Cake

10 to 12 servings

2 cups flour
2 teaspoons baking powder
2 teaspoons cinnamon
1 teaspoon nutmeg
1 teaspoon baking soda
½ teaspoon salt
3 eggs
1¼ cups packed brown sugar
¼ cup honey

¾ cup vegetable oil
½ cup plain or vanilla yogurt
1½ cups shredded unpeeled
   zucchini
1 cup chopped walnuts
½ cup finely diced banana
1 teaspoon grated orange peel

Cream-Cheese Honey Glaze
   (recipe below)

Preheat the oven to 350°F. Stir together flour, baking powder, spices, baking soda, and salt. Set aside. In a large bowl, beat eggs until light. Gradually beat in brown sugar and honey until mixture is light and fluffy. Slowly beat in oil. At low speed of mixer or with rubber spatula, stir in flour mixture alternately with yogurt. Lightly but thoroughly stir in zucchini, walnuts, banana, and orange peel.

Turn batter into a greased, floured, 9- or 10-inch fluted tube pan. Bake 50 to 60 minutes. Cool 10 minutes, then invert on rack and remove from pan. Cool completely. Spread with Cream-Cheese Honey Glaze or confectioners' sugar.

Cream-Cheese Honey Glaze

4 ounces cream cheese
1½ teaspoons orange juice
2 to 3 tablespoons honey
1 teaspoon grated orange peel

In a small bowl, beat the cream cheese with the orange juice. Gradually beat in 2 to 3 tablespoons honey (or to taste). Blend in the orange peel.

Chapter 5

Unfrosted Cakes

Coconut Cake

12 servings

This recipe is a wonderful variation on a traditional pound cake. The buttery richness sets off the coconut to make a treat that will be long remembered. Quick to make, too! Our recipe tester notes that this is the cake her son keeps asking her to make again.

Cake

> 1 pound (4 sticks) butter, softened
> 2 cups sugar
> 2 cups flour, divided
> 6 eggs
> 2¼ cups (7 ounces) unsweetened coconut
> 1 teaspoon vanilla extract

Glaze

> ¼ cup warm water
> ½ cup sugar
> ¼ teaspoon almond extract

To make the cake, preheat the oven to 375°F. Butter and flour a 10-inch tube pan. Cream the butter and sugar. Add 1 cup of the flour. Beat in the eggs one at a time. Add the remaining 1 cup flour and beat. Add the coconut and vanilla and beat until well mixed. Pour into the prepared pan and bake for about 1¼ hours, or until a toothpick inserted in the cake comes out clean. Cool on a wire rack for about 10 minutes before removing from the pan.

To make the glaze, while the cake is still warm, combine the warm water, sugar, and almond extract. Pour slowly over the cake. Cool completely before serving.

Carrie O'Sullivan, Flemington, New Jersey
Hunterdon County 4-H and Agricultural Fair, Flemington, New Jersey

BLUE RIBBON TIP

CREAM THE BUTTER AND SUGAR THOROUGHLY

Many baking recipes start out with the instruction "cream the butter and sugar until light and fluffy." Many of us do this with only moderate energy—after all, everything gets all mixed together in the end, right? Not so. It turns out that this creaming operation incorporates precious bubbles of air into the fat. These bubbles will later be enlarged by the leavening agent (usually baking powder, baking soda, or both), but if the bubbles are not present, the baking powder or soda has nothing to work on, and the cake will not rise very high. For a successful cake, it is essential to cream the butter and sugar thoroughly. In the old days, a pastry chef had to have a very strong arm, but modern appliances make this job easy. You can leave a heavy-duty mixer to cream the butter and sugar while you assemble the other ingredients or grease the pans. It is not possible to do the job quite as well with a handheld mixer. Whatever tools you use, taking time to cream the butter and sugar well will help your cake rise to impressive heights.

Orange Chiffon Cake

12 servings

Our recipe tester called this cake "A#1." It is light, delicious, and very hard to stop eating.

Cake

2¼ cups cake flour
1½ cups sugar, divided
1 teaspoon salt
1 teaspoon baking powder
½ cup vegetable oil
6 egg yolks
¼ cup water
½ cup freshly squeezed orange juice
Zest of 1 orange
1 tablespoon vanilla extract
1 cup egg whites (about 8 egg whites)

Glaze

⅔ cup confectioners' sugar, sifted
2 tablespoons freshly squeezed orange juice
2 teaspoons orange zest

To make the cake, preheat the oven to 325°F. Sift together the flour, ¾ cup of the sugar, salt, and baking powder. In a large bowl, beat the oil, egg yolks, water, orange juice, orange zest, and vanilla. Stir in the dry ingredients and blend well. With clean beaters, beat the egg whites in a large mixing bowl until fluffy. Gradually add the remaining ¾ cup sugar and beat until stiff and glossy but not dry. Stir one-third of the whites into the batter, then carefully fold in the remaining whites. Pour into an ungreased 10-inch tube pan and bake for 1 hour, or until the cake bounces back when touched. Immediately invert the pan over a bottle to hang. When completely cool, remove from the pan.

To make the glaze, stir together all the ingredients until smooth. Brush over the cake.

Robert Markey, Phoenix, Arizona
Arizona State Fair, Phoenix, Arizona

For more recipes and kitchen tips, go to Almanac.com/food.

Cowboy Cobbler

24 servings

This recipe was developed by the cook's grandfather, who was a cowboy. He made it with wild peaches, cooking it in a Dutch oven buried in hot coals. The butter on the bottom is the secret to its melt-in-your-mouth goodness. Apples, pears, nectarines, or other fresh fruits that keep their texture, or even well-drained canned fruit, can be substituted for the peaches.

½ cup (1 stick) butter
1 cup flour
1 cup sugar
½ teaspoon salt
2 teaspoons baking powder
1 cup milk
2 teaspoons vanilla extract
2 to 3 cups peeled and sliced peaches

Preheat the oven to 350°F. Place the butter in a 13x9-inch glass baking dish and place in the oven until the butter is melted (or melt in the microwave and put in the oven to warm). Combine the flour, sugar, salt, and baking powder in a medium bowl. Add the milk and vanilla and mix with a wooden spoon until well blended. Pour over the melted butter. Bake for about 15 minutes, or until the batter has risen. Arrange the peaches on top. Bake until a toothpick inserted in the top comes out clean, about 45 minutes. Serve warm either plain or with ice cream.

Susan Young, Castleton, Vermont
The Old Farmer's Almanac *Recipe Contest, Dublin, New Hampshire*

BLUE RIBBON TIP

★ ★ ★ ★ ★

PEELING PEACHES

To peel peaches, bring a few quarts of water to a boil on the stove. Put the peaches in one or two at a time, remove with a slotted spoon, and plunge into cold water. The peels will slide right off.

Buttermilk Poppy Seed Cake

12 to 14 servings

½ cup poppy seeds
1 cup buttermilk
½ cup (1 stick) butter
½ cup shortening
½ teaspoon vanilla extract
1 cup granulated sugar
½ cup brown sugar
4 eggs, separated
2½ cups flour
1 teaspoon baking powder
1 teaspoon baking soda
1 teaspoon salt

Preheat the oven to 350°F. Lightly grease a nonstick 12-cup Bundt pan. Soak the poppy seeds in the buttermilk for 5 to 8 minutes. In a large bowl, cream the butter, shortening, and vanilla. Beat in the granulated sugar and brown sugar until light and fluffy. Add the egg yolks. Sift together the flour, baking powder, baking soda, and salt. Add to the sugar mixture alternately with the buttermilk, beating after each addition. Beat the egg whites until they are stiff but not dry. Fold half of them into the batter. Gently fold in the remaining whites. Pour into the prepared pan and bake until a toothpick inserted in the cake comes out clean, 35 to 45 minutes. Cool in the pan on a wire rack for 20 minutes, then turn out onto the rack to finish cooling.

Hilda Garey, St. Albans, Vermont
Vermont Dairy Festival, Sheldon, Vermont

Perfect Pound Cake

12 to 16 servings

 2 cups (4 sticks) unsalted butter, softened
 3 cups sugar
 6 eggs
 4 cups flour, sifted
 1 teaspoon baking powder
 ½ teaspoon salt
 1 cup milk
 1 teaspoon lemon extract

Preheat the oven to 300°F. Grease a 12-cup Bundt pan. Cream the butter and sugar until light and fluffy. Add the eggs one at a time, beating well after each addition. Add the flour gradually. Beat in the baking powder, salt, milk, and lemon extract until smooth. Pour into the prepared pan. Bake for 1 hour and 20 minutes, or until a toothpick inserted in the cake comes out clean. Cool in the pan on a wire rack for 10 minutes. Remove from the pan and cool completely on the rack.

Sue Thomas, Indianapolis, Indiana
Indiana State Fair, Indianapolis, Indiana

Pearadise Tart

8 to 10 servings

1 cup firmly packed brown sugar
¼ cup (½ stick) butter, softened
1 egg
½ teaspoon vanilla extract
¾ cup plus 1½ tablespoons cake flour
½ teaspoon baking powder
½ teaspoon salt
1⅓ cups peeled, cored, and finely chopped Bosc pears, divided
    (use firm, ripe pears)
¼ cup walnuts, chopped
⅓ to ½ cup raspberry preserves
1 or 2 Bosc pears, peeled, cored, and thinly sliced
½ teaspoon lemon juice
Fresh mint sprig

Preheat the oven to 375°F. Grease and flour an 8-inch round baking pan. Line the pan with parchment or wax paper. Grease and flour the paper. In a large bowl, cream the brown sugar and butter until light and fluffy. Beat in the egg until smooth, then beat in the vanilla. Sift together the flour, baking powder, and salt. Stir into the batter. Mix in 1 cup of the chopped pears and the walnuts. Pour into the prepared pan and bake for 30 to 35 minutes, or until a toothpick inserted in the center comes out clean. Cool in the pan on a wire rack for 10 minutes. Remove from the pan. Carefully remove the wax paper and cool completely on the rack.

Place the tart on a serving plate. In a small bowl, stir together the preserves and remaining ⅓ cup chopped pears. Spoon over the tart, allowing a little to run over the sides. Arrange the pear slices in the center of the tart. Brush lightly with the lemon juice. Place the mint sprig in the center.

Ashlene Drake, Salem, Oregon
Oregon State Fair and Expo, Salem, Oregon

Plantation Pecan Cake

12 to 20 servings

The prunes in this recipe are its secret ingredient. They subtly improve the flavor while making the texture remarkably tender.

1 cup vegetable oil
2 cups sugar
3 eggs
2 cups flour
1 teaspoon salt
1 teaspoon baking soda
½ teaspoon ground allspice
½ teaspoon ground cinnamon
1 teaspoon ground nutmeg
1 cup buttermilk
1 cup chopped cooked prunes
4 cups coarsely chopped pecans

Preheat the oven to 350°F. Grease a 12-cup Bundt pan. Beat the oil, sugar, and eggs until fluffy. Sift together the flour, salt, baking soda, allspice, cinnamon, and nutmeg. Add to the batter alternately with the buttermilk. Stir in the prunes and pecans. Pour into the prepared pan and bake for 1 hour, or until a toothpick inserted in the cake comes out clean. Cool in the pan for 20 to 30 minutes. Carefully remove from the pan and cool on a wire rack.

Emily James, Boyce, Louisiana
Louisiana Pecan Festival, Colfax, Louisiana

BLUE RIBBON TIP

★ ★ ★ ★

THE PLEASING PECAN

Pecans are unique to the Americas. Many people prefer them to walnuts for baking because they are less bitter. Pecans have the highest fat content of any nut, and this doubtless is one reason we love them so much. The fat in all nuts can cause them to become rancid, however, so any shelled nuts that you plan to store for more than a month should be kept in the freezer.

Cranberry and Pear Butter Crumb Cake

10 to 12 servings

Topping

¾ cup plus 1 tablespoon flour
⅓ cup firmly packed brown sugar
Pinch of salt
¼ cup (½ stick) unsalted butter, melted and cooled

Cake

1 cup (2 sticks) unsalted butter
1 cup firmly packed brown sugar
4 eggs
1 teaspoon vanilla extract
1¾ cups white flour
½ cup whole-wheat flour
1½ teaspoons baking powder
½ teaspoon salt
1 cup fresh cranberries, coarsely chopped
1 firm, ripe pear, peeled, cored, and coarsely chopped
¼ cup granulated sugar
2 teaspoons lemon zest
2 teaspoons lemon juice

To make the topping, combine the flour, brown sugar, and salt in a bowl. Add the butter and cut into the dry ingredients to make damp crumbs. Set aside.

Preheat the oven to 350°F. Butter a 9-inch springform pan.

To make the cake, beat the butter and brown sugar on medium-high for 1 minute. Beat in the eggs one at a time, then beat in the vanilla. Sift the white flour, whole-wheat flour, baking powder, and salt into a separate bowl. Stir the dry ingredients into the creamed mixture in 2 stages, mixing just until the batter is smooth. In a separate bowl, combine the cranberries, pear, granulated sugar, lemon zest, and lemon juice. Fold a little more than half of the fruit mixture into the batter, then spread evenly in the pan. Spread the remaining fruit on top, leaving the edges of the batter uncovered. Scatter the crumb topping evenly over the fruit. Bake for 45 to 50 minutes, or until a

For more recipes and kitchen tips, go to Almanac.com/food.

toothpick inserted in the center comes out clean. Cool in the pan on a wire rack for 15 minutes, then carefully remove the sides of the pan. Slice and serve warm or at room temperature.

Ken Haedrich, Rumney, New Hampshire
Great New England Food Festival, Boston, Massachusetts

★ ★ ★ ★ ★

ZESTIER LEMON

Lemon zest is best made using a zester, a small, inexpensive tool with a little row of holes that remove only the outer, colored part of the rind. Lacking a zester, you can remove strips with a vegetable peeler and then chop them finely. Grated lemon rind often includes part of the pith of the lemon (the white part of the peel just under the yellow), and this can impart a bitter flavor to foods.

Pineapple Cheesecake

10 to 12 servings

Pineapple and cheese make a divine combination, as this unusual recipe demonstrates. Our recipe tester notes, "Yum, yum, yum; this was a personal favorite."

Crust

- 1½ cups graham cracker crumbs
- 3 tablespoons sugar
- ¼ cup (½ stick) butter, melted
- ¼ teaspoon ground cinnamon

Filling

- 2 cups cottage cheese
- 4 eggs
- 3 packages (8 ounces each) cream cheese
- 2 tablespoons flour
- 1 cup sugar
- 1¼ teaspoons vanilla extract
- ¼ teaspoon salt
- 2 cans (20 ounces each) crushed pineapple

Topping

- 2 cups sour cream
- 3 tablespoons sugar

To make the crust, preheat the oven to 300°F. Combine the graham cracker crumbs, sugar, butter, and cinnamon. Press into the bottom and 1½ inches up the sides of a 10-inch springform pan. Bake for 10 minutes. Maintain the oven temperature.

To make the filling, mix the cottage cheese and eggs in a blender. Beat the cream cheese, flour, sugar, vanilla, salt, and cottage cheese mixture until smooth. Drain the pineapple thoroughly. Fold the pineapple into the cream cheese mixture. Pour into the crust. Bake for 1½ hours. Turn the oven off and cool in the oven, with the door ajar, for 1 hour. Remove from the oven.

To make the topping, preheat the oven to 350°F. Combine the sour cream and sugar. Spread over the cheesecake and bake for 10 minutes. Cool slightly and refrigerate until serving time.

Signe Cole, Newport, Maine
Central Maine Egg Festival, Pittsfield, Maine

Chocolate Caramel-Pecan Cheesecake

8 to 10 servings

Crust

- 1 package chocolate wafers
- ½ cup chopped pecans
- ½ cup (1 stick) unsalted butter, melted

Filling

- 3 packages (8 ounces each) cream cheese
- ⅓ cup dark brown sugar
- ¼ cup dark corn syrup
- 2 tablespoons cornstarch
- 3 eggs
- 1 egg yolk

- ⅓ cup sour cream
- 1¼ teaspoons vanilla extract
- 1¾ cups milk chocolate chips
- ½ cup finely chopped pecans

Topping

- ¾ cup milk chocolate chips
- ¼ cup sour cream
- 1 tablespoon brown sugar
- 10 to 12 pecan halves

Caramel Sauce

- 10 or 11 vanilla caramels
- 2 tablespoons sour cream

Preheat the oven to 350°F. To make the crust, finely grind the chocolate wafers with the pecans. Stir in the butter and press into the bottom and up the sides of a 9-inch springform pan.

To make the filling, combine the cream cheese, brown sugar, corn syrup, and cornstarch and beat until smooth. Add the eggs and egg yolk one at a time, beating well after each addition. Stir in the sour cream and vanilla. Melt the chocolate chips and stir into the cream cheese mixture. Fold in the pecans and pour into the crust. Bake for 15 minutes. Turn the oven down to 200°F and bake for 1 hour and 10 minutes, or until the center is no longer shiny. Turn the oven off and let the cake sit in the oven with the door closed for 1 hour. Refrigerate overnight.

To make the topping, melt the chocolate chips. Stir in the sour cream and brown sugar. Spread on top of the cheesecake and top with the pecan halves. Chill thoroughly.

To make the caramel sauce, melt the caramels and stir in the sour cream. Drizzle over the cake before serving.

Robin L. Warchol, Clinton Township, Michigan
Michigan State Fair, Detroit, Michigan

Angel Food Cake

12 to 16 servings

Even people who think they don't like cake usually like this one. We always make it when the accumulation of egg whites in the refrigerator gets unmanageable. It also makes a very welcome addition to any tea table.

12 egg whites
¼ teaspoon salt
1½ teaspoons cream of tartar
1½ cups granulated sugar
1 cup flour
1½ teaspoons vanilla extract

Confectioners' sugar (optional)

Preheat the oven to 375°F. Beat the egg whites until foamy. Add the salt and cream of tartar and beat until soft peaks form. Add the granulated sugar 2 tablespoons at a time and beat until stiff and glossy. Carefully fold in the flour and vanilla. Pour into an ungreased 10-inch tube pan. Bake for 30 to 35 minutes, or until the cake bounces back when gently touched. Invert over a bottle and allow to hang until completely cool. Sprinkle with confectioners' sugar if desired.

Susan Smith, DeSoto, Texas
State Fair of Texas, Dallas, Texas

BLUE RIBBON TIP

★ ★ ★ ★ ★

BEATING THE EGG WHITES INTO SHAPE

C ream of tartar is indispensable to angel food cake. It is often added to egg whites to stabilize them so that they will not lose their volume when they are folded into a batter. In the case of angel food cake, it also helps to stabilize the air bubbles in the batter during the time it is in the oven, so that the cake will hold its shape and not fall. Besides cream of tartar, another good thing for picture-perfect angel food cake is an old-fashioned tool that folds in egg whites or whipped cream extremely well. It has a small (2-inch-square), flat piece of wood with a hole in the middle attached to a handle. Another tool that works well looks like an oval fly swatter, with a much larger mesh. Either will do a good job of folding in egg whites with no loss of volume and no leftover pockets of batter or flour.

Banana Marble Pound Cake

10 to 12 servings

2½ cups sugar
½ cup shortening
½ cup (1 stick) butter, softened
4 eggs
2 medium ripe bananas
1 teaspoon vanilla extract
½ teaspoon lemon extract
3 cups cake flour
½ teaspoon baking soda
¾ cup plus ½ tablespoon buttermilk, divided
⅔ cup mini semisweet chocolate chips
2 tablespoons unsweetened cocoa

Preheat the oven to 325°F. Grease and flour a 10-inch tube pan. Cream the sugar, shortening, and butter until fluffy. Add the eggs one at a time, beating well after each addition. Add the bananas, vanilla, and lemon extract and beat well. Stir together the flour and baking soda and add to the batter alternately with ¾ cup of the buttermilk; beat well. Reserve ⅔ cup batter. Add the chocolate chips to the remaining batter and pour into the prepared pan. Add the cocoa and remaining ½ tablespoon buttermilk to the reserved batter. Drizzle onto the center of the batter in the pan and swirl through with a knife. Bake for 1¼ to 1½ hours, or until a toothpick inserted in the cake comes out clean. Cool in the pan on a wire rack for 10 minutes. Invert and cool completely on the rack.

Sally Crossan, Bear, Delaware
Delaware State Fair, Harrington, Delaware

Cherry Pudding Cake

8 servings

This is a great everyday dessert—who doesn't like cherries?—and it's easier and less expensive than pie.

Cake

½ cup (1 stick) butter
1 cup sugar
2 eggs
½ cup milk
1½ cups flour
2 teaspoons baking powder
½ teaspoon salt
½ teaspoon ground nutmeg
1 can (16 ounces) pitted tart cherries,
    drained (juice reserved)

Sauce

Water
Reserved cherry juice
1 cup sugar
1 tablespoon cornstarch
1 tablespoon butter
Salt
Ground nutmeg

To make the cake, preheat the oven to 350°F. Grease an 8-inch square baking pan. In a large bowl, use an electric mixer to cream the butter and sugar until light and fluffy. Add the eggs and milk and beat until well blended. Combine the flour, baking powder, salt, and nutmeg. Add to the batter and beat well. Gently stir in the cherries and pour into the prepared pan. Bake for 45 to 50 minutes, or until a toothpick inserted in the center comes out clean. Cool slightly in the pan on a wire rack.

To make the sauce, add enough water to the cherry juice to make 2 cups. Combine with the sugar and cornstarch in a small saucepan. Cook over high heat, stirring constantly, until the mixture thickens and bubbles. Turn the heat down and cook for 1 minute, stirring constantly. Remove from the heat and stir in the butter. Add salt and nutmeg to taste. Serve warm over the cake.

Mrs. Guy Hoenke, Traverse City, Michigan
National Cherry Festival, Traverse City, Michigan

Old-Fashioned Gingerbread

6 to 8 servings

½ cup (1 stick) butter or margarine
½ cup sugar
1 egg
1 cup molasses
2½ cups flour
1½ teaspoons baking powder
1 teaspoon ground cinnamon
2 teaspoons ground ginger
½ teaspoon ground cloves
½ teaspoon salt
1 cup hot water
Whipped cream (optional)
Confectioners' sugar (optional)

Preheat the oven to 350°F. Grease an 8- or 9-inch square pan. Cream the butter and sugar until light and fluffy. Beat in the egg and molasses. Sift together the flour, baking powder, cinnamon, ginger, cloves, and salt. Add to the batter alternately with the hot water. Pour into the prepared pan and bake for 35 minutes, or until a toothpick inserted in the center comes out clean. Serve warm with whipped cream or a dusting of confectioners' sugar if desired.

Karen Ritchie, Worthington, Ohio
Ohio State Fair, Columbus, Ohio

For more recipes and kitchen tips, go to Almanac.com/food.

Raspberry-Lemon Pudding Cake

4 to 6 servings

1¼ cups fresh raspberries, or 1 package (10 ounces) frozen berries, thawed
   and drained
1⅓ cups sugar, divided
¼ cup (½ stick) butter, softened
⅓ cup all-purpose flour
¼ teaspoon salt
½ cup freshly squeezed lemon juice
3 eggs, separated
1 cup milk

Preheat the oven to 375°F. Butter a flat-bottomed 2-quart soufflé or baking dish. Set a kettle of water on to boil. Crush the raspberries, add 2 tablespoons of the sugar, and let sit for a few minutes to get juicy.

Cream the butter, gradually adding the remaining sugar. Mix in the flour, salt, and lemon juice. Add the yolks one at a time to the butter mixture; then add the milk. Place the egg whites into a clean mixing bowl. Beat the egg whites until stiff, and fold into the batter.

Pour the raspberries and juice into the prepared dish. Spoon the batter over the top. Set the dish into a deep roasting pan and pour boiling water into the pan to come one-third of the way up the side of the dish. Bake for 45 to 50 minutes, or until the top is firm. The cake separates into two layers while baking—a moist, lemony sponge on top and a raspberry pudding below to spoon over the cake.

Variation:

Raspberry-Orange Pudding Cake: Substitute ½ cup orange juice for the lemon juice, and use 1 cup sugar.

Quick Buttermilk Cake

10 to 12 servings

½ cup (1 stick) butter
1 cup sugar
3 large eggs
1½ cups cake flour
½ teaspoon baking soda
1 teaspoon baking powder
Pinch of salt
¾ cup buttermilk
2 teaspoons minced fresh orange zest

Preheat the oven to 350°F. Butter and flour a 10-cup Bundt pan. Using an electric mixer, cream the butter for 1 minute, then add the sugar slowly, beating constantly at medium speed for 2 minutes. Beat in the eggs. Stop the mixer and add the flour, baking soda, baking powder, pinch of salt, buttermilk, and orange zest. At medium speed, beat 2 minutes longer. Pour the batter into the greased pan and bake for 40 minutes, or until a toothpick inserted into the center of the cake comes out clean. Remove the pan from the oven, place onto a cake rack, and let sit for 10 minutes. Invert the cake on the rack and let it cool completely.

For more recipes and kitchen tips, go to Almanac.com/food.

Variations:

German Sweet Chocolate Cake: Omit the orange zest. Melt a 4-ounce bar of Baker's German Sweet Chocolate in the microwave oven. Let cool slightly. Add the chocolate and 1 teaspoon vanilla extract along with the buttermilk.

Diced Prune and Chocolate Chip Cake: Omit the orange zest if you wish. Finely dice ¼ cup dried prunes and add with ½ cup chocolate chips when you add the buttermilk.

Coconut Cake: Use all-purpose flour. Add 1 cup sweetened coconut along with the flour.

Orange Poppy Seed Cake: Use all-purpose flour. Add ½ cup poppy seeds along with the flour.

Super-Rich Cake: Use all-purpose flour and increase the butter to ¾ cup (1½ sticks).

★ ★ ★ ★

CAKE-BAKING

*A*lways have the ingredients at room temperature. This is especially important for butter, which should be very soft before you use it.

To measure flour, spoon it out of the bag, box, or canister and sprinkle it lightly into a measuring cup. Then, without tapping the cup, level it off with the straight edge of a utensil. Being careless about the way you measure flour can mean the difference between a cake with an excellent texture and one that's incredibly heavy.

The World's Best Cheesecake

10 to 12 servings

Crust

2 cups crushed graham crackers
½ cup (1 stick) butter, melted
¼ cup chopped walnuts

Filling

3 packages (8 ounces each) cream cheese, at room temperature
1½ cups sugar
5 eggs
3 tablespoons lemon juice

Topping

1 pint sour cream
½ cup sugar
1 teaspoon vanilla extract

Preheat the oven to 350°F.

For crust, combine ingredients and press evenly across bottom and sides of a 10-inch springform pan.

For filling, combine cream cheese and sugar. Add eggs one at a time, beating thoroughly after each one. Beat in the lemon juice. Pour filling over crust, and bake for 45 minutes without opening the oven door. Remove cheesecake and reduce heat to 300°F.

For topping, mix ingredients and spread over cheesecake. Return to oven and bake for 15 minutes longer. Cool on rack for several hours, then refrigerate overnight. Serve plain or topped with fresh fruit.

Chapter 6

Fruit Pies

BLUE RIBBON TIP

★ ★ ★ ★ ★

THE PERFECT COOKING APPLE

When a recipe calls for "tart cooking apples," what do you use? There is much debate on this question, and apple growers in Washington think quite differently than those in Michigan, who think differently than those in Vermont and upstate New York. A few varieties that seem to win praise from everyone are Gravenstein, Rhode Island Greening, and pippin, but it's hard to find these if you don't have a specialty orchard nearby. We recommend that you look for McIntosh or Cortland. Opinion is divided on Granny Smith and Golden Delicious, with some cooks claiming that they make the best pies ever and others swearing that they are tasteless and don't cook properly. Try them and come to your own conclusions. The most important factor is that the apples are fresh. Therefore, a variety that is ideal in early fall, such as McIntosh, might not be the best choice in winter, when you might want to consider Northern Spy instead.

In any case, the key to a delicious pie is to use the freshest apples, because storage tends to make apples mushy and bland.

A Great American Apple Pie

8 servings

Amy Fuqua always uses Winesap apples for this pie. She believes that only these apples keep a strong flavor after baking. Many of us can not find Winesaps, so we tried making this with McIntoshes. Although it's probably not quite the same, it sure is good. Amy double-bakes her apples to fit in even more fruit. All the butter she uses to bake the apples keeps them from getting mushy.

Crust

- 2 cups flour
- ½ teaspoon salt
- ¾ cup cold lard
- ¼ cup (½ stick) cold butter
- ⅓ cup ice water (approximately)

Filling

- 12 Winesap apples
- 1 tablespoon lemon juice
- ⅓ cup granulated sugar
- ½ teaspoon ground cinnamon
- ⅛ teaspoon ground nutmeg
- ⅛ teaspoon ground cloves
- 6 tablespoons butter, melted
- ⅓ cup lightly packed brown sugar
- 1 heaping tablespoon cornstarch

To make the crust, combine the flour and salt. Cut in the lard and butter using a pastry blender or food processor. Add just enough ice water for the dough to form a ball. Roll out into 2 circles to fit a 9-inch pie plate, wrap in plastic wrap, and chill for a few hours or overnight.

To make the filling, preheat the oven to 375°F. Peel, core, and dice the apples. Add the lemon juice, sugar, cinnamon, nutmeg, cloves, and butter; mix well. Bake in a covered dish for 40 minutes. Drain the juice from the apples and reserve. Set aside. In a small saucepan, combine the brown sugar, cornstarch, and reserved apple juice. Cook over high heat, stirring constantly, until thick and bubbly. Pour over the apples and stir gently.

Preheat the oven to 450°F. Line a pie plate with one crust. Fill with the apple mixture. Cover with the other crust and crimp to seal. Prick the top crust to make steam vents. Bake for 15 minutes, then reduce the oven temperature to 350°F and bake for 35 minutes more, or until golden brown and bubbly. Cool on a wire rack.

Amy Fuqua, Boulder, Colorado
National Pie Championship, American Pie Council, Lake Forest, Illinois

Blueberry Streusel Pie

8 servings

Some people like this recipe even better than plain blueberry pie, and that's saying quite a lot. Try it for a change.

1 cup sour cream
¾ cup plus 2 tablespoons sugar
1 egg
5 tablespoons flour, divided
1 teaspoon vanilla extract
¼ teaspoon salt
2½ cups fresh or frozen blueberries
1 unbaked 9-inch pie shell
3 tablespoons butter
3 tablespoons pecans, chopped

Preheat the oven to 400°F. Beat the sour cream with ¾ cup of the sugar, egg, 2 tablespoons of the flour, vanilla, and salt for 5 minutes. Fold in the blueberries. Pour into the pie shell and bake for 25 minutes.

Meanwhile, combine the remaining 3 tablespoons flour and 2 tablespoons sugar. Cut in the butter. Stir in the pecans. Sprinkle on the pie and bake for 15 minutes more.

Loleta Dayton, Springfield, Missouri
Ozark Empire Fair, Springfield, Missouri

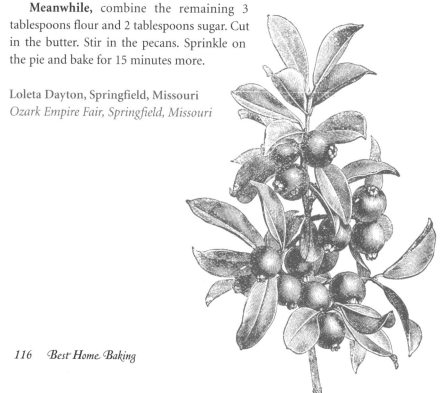

Wild Blueberry Pie

8 servings

This recipe comes from Maine, where wild blueberries grow rampant. Tapioca makes an especially nice thickener for this and other fruit pies.

Crust

2 cups flour
½ teaspoon salt
¾ cup shortening
5 to 6 tablespoons cold water

Filling

⅔ cup sugar
3 tablespoons quick-cooking tapioca
1 teaspoon ground cinnamon
4 cups fresh or frozen wild blueberries
Freshly squeezed lemon juice
1 tablespoon butter or margarine

Preheat the oven to 425°F.

To make the crust, sift together the flour and salt. Cut in the shortening using a pastry blender or food processor. Gradually add the water until the mixture pulls away from the sides of the bowl. Form into a ball and divide in half. Roll each half out into a circle big enough to line a 9-inch pie plate. Line the plate with one circle.

To make the filling, combine the sugar, tapioca, and cinnamon in a large bowl. Add the berries and stir to coat. Pour into the bottom crust. Drizzle with lemon juice and dot with the butter. Place the top crust over the filling, seal the edges, and flute. Pierce the top crust several times to allow steam to escape. Bake for 20 minutes. Reduce the oven temperature to 350°F and bake for 30 minutes more, or until the crust is golden. (Frozen berries may take 10 to 15 minutes longer. You may need to cover the edges with aluminum foil to prevent overbrowning.)

Sue Alimi, Fryeburg, Maine
Fryeburg Fair, Fryeburg, Maine

BLUE RIBBON TIP

★ ★ ★ ★ ★

WILD BLUEBERRIES

Wild blueberries are a specialty of the barrens and mountaintops of Maine. They are much smaller and sweeter than their commercially grown cousins, and they are starting to become available in the frozen food section of many supermarkets. If you can not find wild blueberries and wish to substitute commercial berries, you may need to increase the amount of sugar slightly.

Delicious Rhubarb Pie

8 to 10 servings

Some people forget that there is more to rhubarb than just strawberry-rhubarb pie. This delicious variation combines rhubarb with orange for a sensational taste treat. You may substitute cherry or strawberry juice for the orange juice.

Pastry for double-crust 10-inch pie
4 cups rhubarb cut into ½-inch pieces
⅞ cup sugar
2 tablespoons quick-cooking tapioca
½ cup orange juice
1 tablespoon cornstarch
¼ teaspoon salt
1 egg, beaten
¼ teaspoon ground mace

Preheat the oven to 425°F. Line a pie plate with half the pastry. Place the rhubarb in the bottom crust. Stir together all the remaining ingredients and pour evenly over the rhubarb. Top with the other half of the pastry and seal the edges. Bake for 45 minutes, or until the rhubarb is tender.

Yolanda Bequeath, McDonald, Ohio
Canfield Fair, Canfield, Ohio

BLUE RIBBON TIP

★ ★ ★ ★ ★

MACE AND NUTMEG

Mace and nutmeg are products of the same tree, native to the Moluccas (formerly known as the Spice Islands). That tree is now grown throughout Indonesia and in the Caribbean, particularly in Grenada. The fruit of the tree resembles a peach; its kernel is the nutmeg. Around this kernel grows a red, lacy covering, which is the mace. When the nutmeg is harvested, the fruit is discarded, the mace carefully separated, and the mace and nutmeg dried. Mace is usually somewhat more expensive than nutmeg, and its flavor is more subtle. It has long been appreciated in Europe, and more and more cooks in the United States are beginning to discover its delicate flavor.

Angie's Apple Crumb Pie

8 to 10 servings

Crust

1 cup flour
1 tablespoon sugar
¼ teaspoon salt
1 package (3 ounces) cream cheese, cubed
½ cup (1 stick) unsalted butter, cubed

Filling

⅔ cup sugar
½ teaspoon salt
½ teaspoon ground cinnamon
¼ teaspoon ground cloves
¼ teaspoon ground ginger
6 tart apples, peeled, cored,
   and thinly sliced
2 tablespoons orange juice
2 tablespoons lemon juice
2 tablespoons butter

Topping

½ cup brown sugar
¼ cup granulated sugar
¾ cup flour
½ cup (1 stick) butter, softened
½ cup freshly grated Parmesan cheese

To make the crust, in a large bowl combine the flour, sugar, and salt. With a pastry blender or two knives, cut in the cream cheese and butter until the mixture resembles coarse crumbs. Gently knead the dough into a ball, flatten slightly, cover, and refrigerate for 1 hour. Roll out the dough between 2 sheets of wax paper. Peel off the top paper and invert the crust into a 9-inch pie plate. Refrigerate for at least 1 hour before filling.

Preheat the oven to 350°F.

To make the filling, in a large bowl combine the sugar, salt, cinnamon, cloves, and ginger. Add the apples and sprinkle with the orange and lemon juices. Toss until evenly coated. Pour into the bottom crust and dot with the butter.

To make the topping, in a large bowl combine the brown sugar, granulated sugar, and flour. Work in the butter with your fingertips or a pastry blender until the mixture resembles coarse crumbs. Add the cheese and stir until mixed. Sprinkle over the filling and bake for 50 minutes to 1 hour, or until bubbly.

Angie H. Price, Pembroke, Virginia
The Old Farmer's Almanac *Recipe Contest, Dublin, New Hampshire*

Peach Pie

10 to 12 servings

This prizewinning pie is simple to make, showing that sometimes you can't beat the basics. Serve warm with whipped cream or ice cream.

Pastry for double-crust 9-inch pie
¾ cup sugar
3 tablespoons flour
¼ teaspoon ground cinnamon
Dash of salt
4 cups peeled and sliced peaches
    (about 7 or 8 peaches)
2 tablespoons butter or margarine

Preheat the oven to 400°F. Line a pie plate with half the pastry. Stir together the sugar, flour, cinnamon, and salt. Add the peaches and toss very gently to coat. Pour into the bottom crust and dot with the butter. Top with either a plain or lattice crust made from the other half of the pastry. Sprinkle with a little more sugar and cinnamon. Bake for 40 to 45 minutes, or until the filling is bubbly and the peaches are tender.

Mrs. Howard Cravens, Stonewall, Texas
Peach Jamboree and Rodeo, Stonewall, Texas

Downeast Burgundy Berry Pie

8 to 10 servings

"Downeast" has always been the name of the northeastern coast of Maine, because if you go downwind from Boston, that's where you'll end up. Both blueberries and cranberries grow wild on the starkly beautiful barrens there, and this pie celebrates both flavors.

> **Pastry for double-crust 9-inch pie**
> **1 cup sugar**
> **1 teaspoon ground nutmeg**
> **3½ tablespoons cornstarch**
> **Dash of salt**
> **2 cups fresh or frozen wild blueberries**
> **1½ cups fresh or frozen cranberries**
> **2 tablespoons butter**

Preheat the oven to 400°F. Line a pie plate with half the pastry. Stir together the sugar, nutmeg, cornstarch, and salt. Gently toss with the blueberries and cranberries. Pour into the bottom crust. Dot with the butter. Top with the other half of the pastry and seal. Cut a few slits in the top crust. Bake for 40 to 45 minutes, or until the crust is golden and the filling is bubbly.

Persis Jordan, Machias, Maine
Machias Wild Blueberry Festival, Machias, Maine

For more recipes and kitchen tips, go to Almanac.com/food.

Pear-Almond Pie

8 to 10 servings

Crust

¾ cup almonds, toasted and chopped
1 baked 10-inch pie shell
½ cup almond paste

Filling

⅔ cup sugar
¼ cup cornstarch
¼ teaspoon salt
2 cups half-and-half
1 cup milk
3 egg yolks, slightly beaten
1 tablespoon butter
1½ teaspoons almond extract

Topping

1½ cups water
¾ cup sugar
1 teaspoon grated lemon rind
1 teaspoon vanilla extract
4 pears, peeled, cored, halved, and
    rubbed with lemon juice

1 cup apricot preserves
Whipped cream (optional)
Sliced almonds (optional)

To make the crust, sprinkle the almonds over the pie shell. Break up the almond paste into small bits and sprinkle it over the almonds.

To make the filling, mix the sugar, cornstarch, and salt in a saucepan. Add the half-and-half and milk and whisk to blend. Stirring constantly, bring to a boil over medium-low heat. Reduce the heat to low and cook, stirring constantly, for 1 minute. Gradually stir half of the hot milk mixture into the egg yolks and blend well. Return the mixture to the pan and boil for 2 minutes more, stirring constantly. Remove from the heat and add the butter and almond extract. Press plastic wrap down on top of the custard and cool.

To make the topping, combine the water, sugar, lemon rind, and vanilla in a saucepan and bring to a boil. Stir until the sugar is dissolved, then cover and simmer for 5 minutes. Place the pears cut side down in the syrup and simmer over low heat until they are tender when pierced with a fork, about 10 minutes. Carefully lift from the syrup and drain well. Cool.

Pour the cooled filling into the crust. Arrange the pears in a ring on top of the filling. Melt the apricot preserves over low heat. Press through a strainer to remove any bits of fruit. Lightly brush over the pear halves and filling. Decorate with whipped cream and sliced almonds if desired. Chill for several hours before serving.

Florence Neavoll, Salem, Oregon
Oregon State Fair and Expo, Salem, Oregon

All-American Apple Pie

8 to 10 servings

Is there any cook who does not aspire to making a really mouthwatering apple pie? It is sometimes tempting to search for the "secret ingredient" that will make your pie unique, but it usually turns out that the key to success is the quality of the apples themselves, with the quality of the pastry running a close second. Here is a recipe that we think approaches the ideal.

Crust

- 2 cups flour
- 1 teaspoon salt
- ⅔ cup cold unsalted butter
- 7 tablespoons cold water

Filling

- 7 cups peeled, cored, and thinly sliced tart cooking apples
- 2 tablespoons lemon juice
- 1 cup sugar
- 2 tablespoons flour
- 1 teaspoon ground cinnamon
- ⅛ teaspoon ground nutmeg
- ¼ teaspoon salt
- 2 tablespoons butter

Preheat the oven to 425°F.

To make the crust, sift together the flour and salt. Using a pastry blender, cut in the butter until the mixture is crumbly. Sprinkle on the water, stirring with a fork just until moistened. Form into a ball and divide in half. Roll each half out to a ⅛-inch thickness. Line a 9-inch pie plate with one half of the dough.

To make the filling, in a large bowl toss the apples with the lemon juice. Combine the sugar, flour, cinnamon, nutmeg, and salt. Add the apples and toss gently to coat. Pour into the bottom crust, mounding the apples high in the center. Dot with the butter.

Place the other half of the dough over the filling and fold it under the edge of the bottom crust. Press the edges together to seal, then crimp. Make at least 3 slits in the top to vent the steam. If desired, decorate with pastry scraps cut in the shape of apples. Bake for 45 to 50 minutes, or until the apples are fork-tender and the crust is golden brown. Cool on a wire rack.

Jean Thomas, Buchanan, Virginia
Salem Fair, Salem, Virginia

Schnappsy Peach Pie

10 servings

Because this crust calls for more shortening than usual, it is almost a shortbread—different and delicious.

Crust

3 cups flour
1 teaspoon salt
1½ cups (3 sticks) butter or
    butter-flavored shortening
1 egg
1 tablespoon white vinegar
5 tablespoons cold water

Filling

¾ cup granulated sugar
½ cup packed brown sugar
2 tablespoons flour

½ teaspoon ground cinnamon
¼ teaspoon ground nutmeg
⅛ teaspoon ground cardamom
1½ cups peeled, cored, and sliced
    apples (about 3 apples)
1½ cups peeled and sliced peaches
    (about 3 peaches)
⅓ cup walnuts, chopped
1 teaspoon grated orange rind
½ teaspoon grated lemon rind
¼ cup peach schnapps
2 tablespoons butter

Preheat the oven to 375°F.

To make the crust, sift together the flour and salt. Add the butter or shortening and mix with a pastry blender. Beat the egg with the vinegar and water. Add to the dough and mix until it forms a ball. Divide in half and roll each half out into a circle large enough to line a 9-inch pie plate with a 1-inch overhang. Line the plate with one circle.

To make the filling, combine the granulated sugar, brown sugar, flour, cinnamon, nutmeg, and cardamom. Add the apples, peaches, walnuts, and grated orange and lemon rinds. Pour into the bottom crust. Pour the schnapps over the filling and dot with the butter. Cut out a design in the top crust if desired. Fold the crust gently in half and lift onto the filling. Unfold and crimp the edges together, trimming any excess. Bake for 12 minutes, then reduce the oven temperature to 350°F. Bake for 50 minutes more, or until the fruit is tender.

Darlene R. Lamp, Manning, Iowa
The Old Farmer's Almanac *Recipe Contest, Dublin, New Hampshire*

Cherry Pie

8 to 10 servings

David Oxley has made this blue ribbon winner dozens of times. His friends always request it for potluck suppers and special occasions, and even people who don't usually eat cherry pie say that they like this one.

Crust

- 2 cups flour
- 1 teaspoon salt
- ⅔ cup shortening
- 5 to 7 tablespoons ice water

Filling

- 2 cans (16 ounces each) tart red cherries packed in water
- 1½ cups sugar, divided
- ⅓ cup cornstarch
- Dash of salt
- 1 tablespoon butter
- 4 drops almond extract

- Milk
- Sugar for sprinkling

Preheat the oven to 375°F.

To make the crust, stir together the flour and salt. Cut in the shortening with a pastry blender or food processor. Sprinkle the water over the mixture 1 tablespoon at a time, tossing with a fork after each addition. Add just enough water to moisten the dough. Form into a ball and divide in half. Roll each half out to fit a 9-inch pie plate. Line the plate with one half.

To make the filling, drain the cherries, reserving 1 cup of the juice. Combine ¾ cup of the sugar, cornstarch, and salt in a saucepan. Slowly add the reserved juice, stirring thoroughly to combine. Cook over medium heat, stirring constantly, until boiling. Continue cooking and stirring for 1 minute. Remove from the heat and mix in the butter and remaining ¾ cup sugar; stir to dissolve. Stir in the cherries and almond extract. Pour into the bottom crust. Cut the other half of the crust into ¾-inch-wide strips and weave into a lattice top. Crimp the edges. Brush the top with milk and sprinkle with sugar. Bake for 50 to 60 minutes, or until the top is nicely browned and the filling is thick and bubbly. Cool on a wire rack.

David Oxley, Seattle, Washington
Western Washington Fair, Puyallup, Washington

Cranberry Pie

8 to 10 servings

2 cups chopped cranberries
1 cup chopped pecans
1½ cups sugar, divided
2 large eggs
½ cup (1 stick) butter, melted and cooled
1 cup flour
¼ teaspoon salt
2 teaspoons vanilla extract

Preheat the oven to 350°F. In a greased 10-inch pie plate, combine the cranberries, pecans, and ½ cup of the sugar. Stir gently to mix well. In a mixing bowl, combine the eggs, melted butter, remaining 1 cup sugar, flour, salt, and vanilla. Stir the batter until it is smooth and all the flour is mixed in. Pour the batter over the cranberry mixture and stir gently with a spoon to partly incorporate the top and bottom layers; they don't need to be completely blended. Bake for about 40 minutes, or until done.

Ginger Peach Pie

6 to 8 servings

2 cups crushed gingersnaps
3 tablespoons butter, melted
1 egg, separated
3 tablespoons flour
1½ cups half-and-half
⅓ cup sugar
3 tablespoons finely chopped candied ginger,
    or 1 tablespoon grated fresh gingerroot
1 teaspoon vanilla extract
4 medium peaches, peeled and sliced
⅓ cup seedless raspberry jam or jelly

Preheat the oven to 350°F. Combine the crushed gingersnaps, melted butter, and egg white in a medium bowl and mix well with a fork. Let sit for 5 minutes. Press the mixture into a 9-inch pie pan, using your fingers to smooth it and evenly cover the bottom and sides. Bake for 5 minutes. Check the crust, smooth the edges up if they are sagging, and bake for 5 minutes longer.

While the crust is baking, combine the flour and ¼ cup of the half-and-half in a heavy saucepan to make the custard. Stir with a whisk until smooth. Put the pan over medium-low heat and add the remaining half-and-half in a thin stream, whisking constantly. Stir in the sugar and continue to cook, stirring constantly, until the mixture begins to thicken. Continue cooking and stirring, not letting it boil, until it is as thick as pudding. Add a table-spoon or two of hot mixture to the egg yolk, stir well, and add the egg yolk to the hot mixture. Continue to cook for a few more min-utes. Remove from heat and stir in the ginger and vanilla. Let cool slightly. Pour the mixture into the baked crust and chill.

Arrange the sliced peaches over the custard. Melt the jam or jelly in a small saucepan and brush over the peaches. Chill for 2 to 3 hours and serve.

For more recipes and kitchen tips, go to Almanac.com/food.

Chapter 7

Custard & Cream Pies

Coconut-Banana Cream Pie

8 servings

This recipe combines two unbeatable flavors for a dessert that leaves no question in your mind as to why it won both first place and an award of excellence.

Crust

   3 cups sweetened coconut
   7 tablespoons butter or margarine

Filling

   ¾ cup sugar
   ¼ cup flour
   3 tablespoons cornstarch
   ¼ teaspoon salt
   3 cups light cream
   4 egg yolks, slightly beaten
   2 teaspoons vanilla extract
   2 large, firm bananas, sliced

   1 cup whipped cream (optional)
   Sliced bananas (optional)

To make the crust, preheat the oven to 350°F. In a skillet, sauté the coconut in the butter until golden. Press all but 2 tablespoons into the bottom and up the sides of a greased 9-inch pie plate. Bake for 7 minutes.

To make the filling, combine the sugar, flour, cornstarch, and salt in a saucepan. Whisk in the cream and egg yolks and gradually bring to a boil over medium-low heat, stirring constantly. Boil for 2 minutes, stirring constantly. Remove from the heat and stir in the vanilla. Cool to room temperature. Place the 2 sliced bananas in the crust and cover with the custard. Chill until set, about 2 hours. Sprinkle with the 2 tablespoons coconut reserved from the crust. If desired, garnish with whipped cream and sliced bananas.

Melba Daniel, Hawkinsville, Georgia
Georgia National Fair, Perry, Georgia

Cranberry-Walnut Chess Pie

8 servings

The origin of the name "chess pie," traditionally associated with the South, is shrouded in mystery. One theory says that it is a variant of "Jes' pie!" ("Just pie!") In any case, this version is an especially good one, as the tartness of the cranberries cuts the sweetness of this very rich treat.

1 cup fresh or frozen cranberries, chopped
1¼ cups sugar, divided
½ cup (1 stick) butter, softened
3 tablespoons flour
3 egg yolks
⅛ teaspoon salt
⅔ cup evaporated milk
1 teaspoon vanilla extract
½ cup walnuts, chopped
1 unbaked 8-inch pie shell

Preheat the oven to 375°F. Combine the cranberries and ¼ cup of the sugar and set aside. Beat the butter and the remaining 1 cup sugar until well blended. Add the flour, egg yolks, salt, and evaporated milk and beat. Stir in the cranberries, vanilla, and walnuts. Pour into the pie shell. Bake for 45 minutes, or until the center is still soft but almost set. Cool thoroughly on a wire rack.

Derolyn St. Louis, Freetown, Massachusetts
Cranberry Harvest Festival, East Wareham, Massachusetts

Pumpkin-Butterscotch Mousse Pie

8 servings

Butterscotch complements the flavor of pumpkin, and this recipe presents a delicious alternative to traditional pumpkin pie.

Crust

- 1¾ cups sweetened coconut
- ½ cup graham cracker crumbs
- ¼ cup (½ stick) butter or margarine, melted

- 1 package (12 ounces) butterscotch chips, divided

Filling

- 1 envelope unflavored gelatin
- ⅓ cup apple juice or water
- 1 package (3 ounces) cream cheese, softened
- ⅓ cup plus 1 tablespoon sugar, divided
- 1¼ cups solid-pack pumpkin
- ½ teaspoon pumpkin pie spice
- ¾ cup heavy cream

Whipped cream (optional)

To make the crust, preheat the oven to 300°F. Combine the coconut and graham cracker crumbs in a medium bowl. Add the butter and mix until moistened. Press into the bottom and up the sides of a 9-inch pie plate. Bake for 20 to 25 minutes, or until golden brown.

Melt ½ cup of the butterscotch chips in a small, heavy saucepan over low heat. Spread thinly on the bottom of the crust. Chill.

To make the filling, soften the gelatin in the juice or water for 5 minutes. Heat gently over low heat until the gelatin is dissolved. Cool. Melt 1 cup butterscotch chips; cool slightly. In a large bowl, beat the cream cheese and ⅓ cup of the sugar until fluffy. Gradually beat in the gelatin mixture, melted butterscotch, pumpkin, and pumpkin pie spice. Chill until slightly thickened. Beat the cream with the remaining 1 tablespoon sugar until stiff peaks form. Fold into the pumpkin mixture. Spoon into the crust. Chill for at least 3 hours or overnight.

Before serving, melt the remaining ½ cup butterscotch chips. Thin as necessary with a little cream. Spoon into a small plastic bag. Snip a small corner from the bag and drizzle the butterscotch over the chilled pie. Add rosettes of whipped cream around the edge if desired.

Paula Rassi, Morton, Illinois
Morton Pumpkin Festival, Morton, Illinois

For more recipes and kitchen tips, go to Almanac.com/food.

Pecan Custard Pie

10 servings

This is an interesting variation on traditional pecan pie. For people who like their pies light and fluffy, this slips right down.

- 1 envelope unflavored gelatin
- ½ teaspoon salt
- ¾ cup dark brown sugar
- 4 eggs, separated
- ½ cup (½ stick) butter or margarine, divided
- 1 cup milk
- 1 teaspoon vanilla
- 1 cup pecans, chopped
- ½ cup granulated sugar
- 1 baked 9-inch pie shell
- ½ cup heavy cream, whipped

Combine the gelatin, salt, and brown sugar in the top of a double boiler. Heat slightly over hot, not boiling, water. Stir in the egg yolks, 2 tablespoons of the butter, and milk. Cook, stirring occasionally, until slightly thickened. Remove from the heat and add the vanilla. Cool, then chill in the refrigerator, stirring occasionally.

Sauté the pecans in the remaining 2 tablespoons butter, taking care not to burn the butter, until browned. Drain on paper towels. Beat the egg whites and granulated sugar until stiff peaks form. When the custard is thickened to the point where it mounds slightly when stirred with a spoon, fold in the egg whites and half the pecans. Pour into the pie shell and chill until firm to the touch. Top with the whipped cream and sprinkle with the remaining pecans.

Margaret Burlew, Houma, Louisiana
Louisiana Pecan Festival, Colfax, Louisiana

Editor's note: If you are concerned about using raw egg whites, try substituting prepared eggs whites found in the dairy case or egg white powder.

Chocolate-Rum Chiffon Pie

10 servings

Crust

- 1½ cups chocolate graham cracker crumbs
- 2 tablespoons sugar
- Pinch of salt
- ½ cup (1 stick) butter, melted

Filling

- 1 envelope unflavored gelatin
- 1 cup coffee, at room temperature
- ½ cup milk
- 2 squares (2 ounces) unsweetened chocolate, coarsely chopped
- ½ cup sugar, divided
- ¼ teaspoon salt
- 3 eggs, separated
- 2 tablespoons rum
- 1 teaspoon vanilla extract
- 1 cup whipping cream

To make the crust, preheat the oven to 325°F. Combine the graham cracker crumbs, sugar, and salt in a mixing bowl and toss together. Add the butter and stir vigorously until blended. Press the mixture into the bottom and up the sides of a 9-inch pie plate. Bake for 8 minutes. Cool completely.

To make the filling, sprinkle the gelatin over the coffee and let stand for a few minutes. In a saucepan, combine the milk and chocolate. Cook over low heat, stirring constantly, until the chocolate melts. Remove from the heat. Add ¼ cup of the sugar, salt, and egg yolks and whisk until well blended. Return to moderate heat and cook, stirring constantly, until the mixture thickens slightly and barely reaches a simmer, about 5 minutes. Do not boil. Add the softened gelatin and cook, stirring constantly, for about 1 minute more. Stir in the rum and vanilla. Pour into a bowl and chill, stirring occasionally, until it mounds when dropped from a spoon, about 1 hour.

Whip the cream until stiff. In another bowl, with clean beaters, beat the egg whites until soft peaks form. Fold the cream and egg whites into the chocolate mixture and pile into the crust. Chill for several hours before serving.

Kate Stewart Rovner, Plano, Texas
State Fair of Texas, Dallas, Texas

Editor's note: If you are concerned about using raw egg whites, try substituting prepared eggs whites found in the dairy case or egg white powder.

Lemon Sponge Pie

10 servings

Of this "Best of Show" pie, our recipe tester says enthusiastically, "I'll definitely be making this one again."

Crust

- 1 cup flour
- ½ teaspoon salt
- ⅓ cup shortening
- 2 tablespoons cold milk

Filling

- 3 tablespoons butter or margarine, softened
- 1¼ cups sugar
- 4 eggs, separated
- 3 tablespoons flour
- Dash of salt
- 1¼ cups milk
- Grated rind of 2 lemons
- ⅓ cup lemon juice

To make the crust, combine the flour and salt. Cut in the shortening until the mixture resembles coarse meal. Stir in the milk and form the dough into a ball. Roll out on a lightly floured surface to an 11-inch circle. Line a 9-inch pie plate with the dough and crimp the edges. Set aside.

To make the filling, preheat the oven to 375°F. In a large mixing bowl, cream the butter and sugar until fluffy. Beat in the egg yolks, flour, salt, milk, lemon rind, and lemon juice. In a small bowl, with clean beaters, beat the egg whites until stiff but not dry. Fold into the lemon mixture. Pour into the crust. Bake for 15 minutes. Reduce the oven temperature to 300°F and bake for 45 minutes more, or until the top is golden and a toothpick inserted in the center comes out clean. Cool on a wire rack.

Shirley M. Casity, New Springfield, Ohio
Canfield Fair, Canfield, Ohio

Coffee Cream Pie with Chocolate Crust

8 to 12 servings

Crust

¼ cup (½ stick) unsalted butter
⅔ cup semisweet chocolate chips
1⅓ cups graham cracker crumbs

Filling

¼ cup instant coffee powder
2 tablespoons boiling water
1¼ cups milk
4 egg yolks
½ cup plus 2 tablespoons sugar, divided
3 tablespoons cornstarch
½ tablespoon unsalted butter
1 cup cold heavy cream
1 tablespoon semisweet chocolate chips, finely chopped

To make the crust, preheat the oven to 375°F. Generously butter a 9- or 10-inch pie plate. Melt the butter and chocolate chips in the top of a double boiler. Stir to mix well. In a bowl, combine with the graham cracker crumbs. Press firmly into the bottom and up the sides of the pie plate. Place in the freezer for 10 minutes. Remove from the freezer and bake for 8 minutes. Cool completely on a wire rack.

To make the filling, dissolve the coffee in the boiling water (this will be extra strong) and let sit for 15 minutes. Combine with the milk in a medium saucepan and heat until hot but not boiling. Meanwhile, in a large bowl beat the egg yolks, ½ cup of the sugar, and cornstarch until light and creamy. Slowly whisk in the hot milk until blended. Return to the saucepan and bring to a boil, whisking constantly. Boil for 1 minute. Pour into a bowl and stir in the butter. Place plastic wrap directly on the surface of the custard. Chill for about 1 hour. Whisk until smooth and light in color.

Beat the cream with the remaining 2 tablespoons sugar until fluffy and fully whipped. Fold about 1½ cups whipped cream into the custard. Spoon into the crust. Sprinkle with the finely chopped chocolate chips. Force the remaining whipped cream through a pastry tube or bag to decorate the pie. Chill for at least 4 hours. Let stand at room temperature for 15 minutes before serving.

Jeanne Lemlin, Great Barrington, Massachusetts
Great New England Food Festival, Boston, Massachusetts

For more recipes and kitchen tips, go to Almanac.com/food.

Irish Potato Pie

8 to 10 servings

This recipe, with slight adjustments, was brought over "on the boat" by the cook's great-great-aunt shortly after a potato famine in the 1880s. When asked why she had brought a potato pie (rather than a fruit pie) recipe with her, she'd answer that she had hoped that America would have an abundant supply of potatoes, as in Ireland there was "nary a sound potato to be had there. May God bring them back." Of course, God did, and we celebrate that with the fine legacy of Aunt Bridget's potato custard pie.

3 eggs
2 cups half-and-half or light cream
2 cups mashed potatoes (whipped smooth with no lumps)
1 cup sugar
1 teaspoon vanilla extract
¼ teaspoon salt
1 tablespoon Irish whiskey, brandy, or sherry (optional)
1 unbaked 10-inch deep-dish pie shell with high fluted edge
Freshly grated nutmeg
Toasted slivered almonds

Preheat the oven to 350°F. In a mixing bowl, beat the eggs slightly. Stir in the half-and-half or cream, potatoes, sugar, vanilla, salt, and liquor (if using). Beat well until smooth. Cover the fluted edge of the pie shell with aluminum foil to prevent over-browning. Pour the filling into the shell and sprinkle with nutmeg. Place on the center rack of the oven and bake for 40 minutes. Remove the foil and bake for 15 to 18 minutes more, or until a toothpick inserted in the center comes out clean. Cool on a wire rack. Sprinkle the almonds around the outer edge and dust with additional nutmeg. Serve at room temperature; store in the refrigerator.

Mary Cummings, New Smyrna Beach, Florida
The Old Farmer's Almanac *Recipe Contest, Dublin, New Hampshire*

Sweet Potato Pecan Pie

10 to 12 servings

This recipe won Raven Stocks first place in pies in the youth division. It tastes like a fancy pumpkin pie—perfect for a special holiday treat.

Filling

1 pound sweet potatoes (about 2 potatoes), cooked and peeled
¼ cup (½ stick) butter or margarine
1 can (14 ounces) sweetened condensed milk
1 teaspoon vanilla extract
1 teaspoon ground cinnamon
½ teaspoon ground nutmeg
½ teaspoon salt
2 eggs
1 unbaked 9-inch pie shell

Topping

1 egg
3 tablespoons light corn syrup
3 tablespoons light-brown sugar
1 tablespoon butter or margarine, melted
½ tablespoon maple flavoring
1 cup pecans, chopped

Preheat the oven to 350°F.

To make the filling, in a large bowl beat the hot sweet potatoes and butter until smooth. Beat in all the remaining filling ingredients. Pour into the pie shell. Bake for 30 minutes. Maintain the oven temperature.

To make the topping, beat together all the topping ingredients. Pour over the filling. Bake for 20 minutes more. Cool completely on a wire rack.

Raven Stocks, Tabor City, North Carolina
North Carolina Yam Festival, Tabor City, North Carolina

Lemon Meringue Pie

10 to 12 servings

Crust
- 1 cup flour
- ¼ teaspoon salt
- ⅓ cup butter
- 3 to 4 tablespoons ice water

Meringue
- 5 or 6 egg whites
- ¼ teaspoon cream of tartar
- 6 tablespoons sugar
- ½ teaspoon vanilla extract

Filling
- 1½ cups sugar
- ⅓ cup plus 1 tablespoon cornstarch
- ¼ teaspoon salt
- 1½ cups water
- 3 egg yolks, slightly beaten
- Grated rind of 2 lemons
- ½ cup freshly squeezed lemon juice
- 3 tablespoons butter

To make the crust, preheat the oven to 425°F. Combine the flour and salt. Cut in the butter using a pastry blender or food processor. Gradually add water until the dough forms a ball. Roll out to fit a 9-inch pie plate. Line the pie plate with the dough. Crimp the edges and prick the bottom. Line the crust with aluminum foil and dried beans or pie weights. Bake for 10 minutes. Remove the foil and weights. Bake for 10 minutes more. Cool on a wire rack.

To make the filling, stir together the sugar, cornstarch, and salt in a medium saucepan. Whisk in the water and egg yolks. Bring to a boil over medium-low heat, stirring constantly. Boil for 1 minute. Remove from the heat and stir in the lemon rind, lemon juice, and butter. Pour into the crust.

To make the meringue, preheat the oven to 400°F. Beat the egg whites and cream of tartar until foamy. Gradually add the sugar and beat until stiff but not dry. Fold in the vanilla. Heap over the filling, being sure to bring the meringue well over the edges of the crust. Bake for about 10 minutes, or until lightly browned.

Kate Thomas, Fitzwilliam, New Hampshire
The Old Farmer's Almanac *Recipe Contest, Dublin, New Hampshire*

Date Delight

8 servings

2 cups graham cracker crumbs, divided
¼ cup (½ stick) butter, melted
¾ cup sugar, divided
2 slightly heaping tablespoons cornstarch
⅛ teaspoon salt
2 cups milk
2 eggs, separated
8 ounces dates, finely chopped
1 teaspoon vanilla extract
1 cup walnuts or pecans, chopped

Whipped cream (optional)

Preheat the oven to 350°F. Reserve ½ cup graham cracker crumbs. Combine the remaining crumbs and butter and press into the bottom and up the sides of a 9-inch glass pie plate. Mix together ½ cup of the sugar, cornstarch, and salt in a saucepan. Whisk in the milk and egg yolks. Bring to a boil over medium-low heat, stirring constantly. Boil for 1 minute. Cool. Pour into the crust and sprinkle the dates on top.

Beat the egg whites until soft peaks form. Gradually add the remaining ¼ cup sugar and beat until stiff peaks form. Fold in the vanilla. Spread on top of the dates. Sprinkle with the nuts and reserved graham cracker crumbs. Bake for 30 to 40 minutes, or until golden brown. Chill overnight. Serve with whipped cream if desired.

Connie Harlow, Indio, California
National Date Festival, Indio, California

Pumpkin Pie

6 to 8 servings

Pumpkin pie, popular since Colonial days (but formerly called pumpkin pudding), can also be made with winter squash—in fact, some folks prefer it that way!

2 cups pumpkin purée
⅔ cup brown sugar
⅓ cup granulated sugar
1 tablespoon flour
½ teaspoon salt
1 teaspoon cinnamon
½ teaspoon grated nutmeg
½ teaspoon ginger
¼ teaspoon allspice
Pinch of black pepper
1 cup light cream
⅓ cup milk
2 eggs, beaten
1 teaspoon vanilla extract
1 pie shell (9- or 10-inch)

Preheat the oven to 400°F. Prebake the piecrust for about 6 minutes; allow to cool. Maintain oven temperature. In a large bowl, combine all pie-filling ingredients and stir with a large whisk until smooth. Pour mixture into partially baked pie shell. Bake for about 45 minutes, until filling is set but still slightly wobbly in the center. Cool pie on a wire rack. Serve with whipped cream or ice cream.

Southern Sweet Potato Pie

1 pie

⅓ cup butter
¾ cup sugar
2 eggs, beaten
2 cups mashed sweet potatoes (if using canned sweet potatoes, do not use
    ones packed in syrup)
¾ cup evaporated milk
1 teaspoon vanilla extract
½ teaspoon grated nutmeg
½ teaspoon cinnamon
¼ teaspoon salt
1 unbaked 9-inch pie shell

Preheat the oven to 375°F. Cream butter and sugar together. Add eggs and stir. Add sweet potatoes and mix well. Stir in milk, vanilla, nutmeg, cinnamon, and salt, making sure all ingredients are thoroughly mixed. Pour into pie shell and bake for 40 minutes. When using a store-bought pie shell, use a 9-inch deep-dish shell.

Chapter 8

Bars & Brownies

Pumpkin Cheesecake Bars

16 to 32 bars

These nice little treats are almost like individual pumpkin pies, but a bit creamier because of the cream cheese.

- 1 cup flour
- ⅓ cup loosely packed brown sugar
- ¼ cup (½ stick) butter, softened
- ½ cup pecans or walnuts, finely chopped
- 1 package (8 ounces) cream cheese
- ¾ cup granulated sugar
- ½ cup solid-pack pumpkin
- 2 eggs, slightly beaten
- 1 teaspoon vanilla extract
- 1½ teaspoons ground cinnamon
- 1 teaspoon ground allspice

Preheat the oven to 350°F. Combine the flour and brown sugar in a bowl. Cut in the butter to make a crumb mixture. Stir in the nuts. Set aside ¼ cup of this mixture. Press the remaining mixture into the bottom of an ungreased 8-inch square pan. Bake for 15 minutes. Cool slightly. Maintain the oven temperature.

Combine the cream cheese, granulated sugar, pumpkin, eggs, vanilla, cinnamon, and allspice in a bowl and blend until smooth. Pour over the baked crust. Sprinkle with the reserved crumbs. Bake for 30 to 35 minutes. Cool, then cut into bars.

Deborah Taylor, Keene, New Hampshire
Great Gourd Bake-off, Keene, New Hampshire

Lemony Hazelnut Bars

20 bars

⅓ cup butter, softened
1 cup sugar, divided
1 cup plus 2 tablespoons flour, divided
½ cup ground toasted hazelnuts, divided (see tip on page 73)
2 eggs
½ teaspoon baking powder
2 teaspoons grated lemon rind
3 tablespoons freshly squeezed lemon juice
Confectioners' sugar

Preheat the oven to 350°F. Beat the butter with an electric mixer for about 30 seconds. Add ¼ cup of the sugar and beat until combined. Beat in 1 cup of the flour and ¼ cup of the hazelnuts. Press into an ungreased 8-inch square pan. Bake for about 10 minutes, or until lightly browned. Maintain the oven temperature.

Combine the eggs, remaining ¾ cup sugar, remaining 2 tablespoons flour, baking powder, lemon rind, and lemon juice. Beat for 2 minutes, making sure that the mixture is thoroughly combined. Pour over the hot crust and sprinkle the remaining ¼ cup hazelnuts on top. Bake for 20 minutes more, or until lightly browned. Cool completely, sprinkle with confectioners' sugar, and cut into bars.

Ellen West, South Deerfield, Massachusetts
Franklin County Fair, Greenfield, Massachusetts

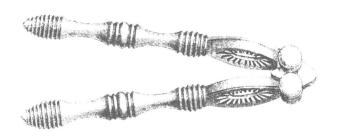

Triple-Good Bars

4 dozen bars

2 cups raisins
1 can (14 ounces) sweetened condensed milk
1 tablespoon grated lemon rind
1 tablespoon lemon juice
1 cup (2 sticks) butter or margarine, softened
1⅓ cups firmly packed brown sugar
1½ teaspoons vanilla extract
1 cup flour
½ teaspoon baking soda
¼ teaspoon salt (optional)
2½ cups quick-cooking or old-fashioned oats
1½ cups chopped walnuts

Preheat the oven to 375°F. Grease a 13x9-inch baking pan.

In a medium saucepan, combine the raisins, condensed milk, lemon rind, and lemon juice. Cook over medium heat, stirring constantly, just until the mixture begins to bubble. Remove from the heat and cool slightly.

Beat the butter, brown sugar, and vanilla until fluffy. Add the flour, baking soda, salt (if using), oats, and walnuts. Blend until evenly mixed and crumbly. Press half of this mixture into the prepared pan. Spread the raisin mixture to within ½ inch of the edge. Sprinkle with the remaining oat mixture and pat lightly. Bake for 25 to 30 minutes, or until golden brown. Cool completely, then cut into bars.

Carolyn Moreton, Flemington, New Jersey
Hunterdon County 4-H and Agricultural Fair, Flemington, New Jersey

Peanut Butter Bars

3 to 4 dozen bars

Peanut butter and chocolate are always a winning combination. These bars make an unbeatable lunch box treat.

Bars

    ½ cup (1 stick) butter or margarine, softened
    ½ cup crunchy peanut butter
    ½ cup loosely packed brown sugar
    ½ cup granulated sugar
    1 egg
    1 teaspoon vanilla extract
    1 cup flour
    ½ cup quick-cooking or old-fashioned oats
    1 teaspoon baking soda
    ¼ teaspoon salt
    1 cup semisweet chocolate chips

Icing

    ½ cup confectioners' sugar
    2 tablespoons creamy peanut butter
    2 tablespoons milk

To make the bars, preheat the oven to 350°F. Grease a 13x9-inch baking pan. In a mixing bowl, combine the butter, crunchy peanut butter, brown sugar, and granulated sugar. Add the egg and vanilla and mix well. In another bowl, combine the flour, oats, baking soda, and salt. Stir into the peanut butter mixture. Spread in the prepared pan. Sprinkle with the chocolate chips. Bake for 20 to 25 minutes, or until lightly browned. Cool for 10 minutes.

To make the icing, combine all the ingredients and drizzle over the uncut bars. Cool completely before cutting into bars.

Sharon Fish, Morrisville, Missouri
Ozark Empire Fair, Springfield, Missouri

Decadent Brownies

1 dozen brownies

Brownies

> 15 ounces fine European semisweet chocolate
> ¾ cup (1½ sticks) unsalted butter
> ¾ cup confectioners' sugar
> 2 tablespoons flour
> 4 eggs, separated
> 1 teaspoon vanilla extract
> ¾ cup sour cream

Glaze

> ¼ cup (½ stick) unsalted butter
> 4 ounces fine European semisweet chocolate
> 1½ cups confectioners' sugar
> 3 tablespoons boiling water or strong coffee
> 2 teaspoons vanilla extract

To make the brownies, preheat the oven to 375°F. Lightly grease a 9-inch square glass baking dish. Melt the chocolate and butter in a large saucepan. Whisk in the confectioners' sugar and flour and remove from the heat. Add the egg yolks one at a time, beating well after each addition. Stir in the vanilla. Beat the egg whites in a separate bowl until stiff, then fold into the chocolate mixture. Remove 1 cup of this mixture and blend with the sour cream; set aside. Pour the chocolate-egg mixture into the prepared pan. Top with the chocolate-sour cream mixture and swirl with a knife. Bake for 30 minutes. Cool completely.

To make the glaze, melt the butter and chocolate together. Remove from the heat and beat in the confectioners' sugar, water or coffee, and vanilla. Spread over the cooled brownies.

Jill Anderson, Perry, Georgia
Georgia National Fair, Perry, Georgia

Apricot-Almond Bars

4 dozen bars

This recipe makes a very fancy-looking bar, suitable for holidays and the most elegant occasions.

Topping

1½ cups sugar
3 cups sliced almonds
4 egg whites (2 yolks reserved
    for crust)
2 tablespoons flour
½ teaspoon ground cinnamon
¼ teaspoon freshly grated nutmeg

Crust

2½ cups flour
½ cup sugar
1 cup (2 sticks) butter
2 egg yolks

Apricot Glaze

½ cup apricot preserves
1 tablespoon water

Chocolate Glaze

3 squares (3 ounces) semisweet
    chocolate
1 square (1 ounce) unsweetened
    chocolate

To make the topping, combine all the ingredients in the top of a double boiler. Cook, stirring occasionally, until the mixture reaches 110°F on a candy thermometer. Set aside.

To make the crust, preheat the oven to 350°F. Line a 15x10-inch jelly-roll pan with aluminum foil. Combine the flour and sugar. Cut in the butter. Add the egg yolks and mix well. Press into the prepared pan. Bake for 15 minutes. Spread the topping over the crust and bake for 20 minutes more.

To make the apricot glaze, melt the apricot preserves with the water in a small saucepan. Brush over the topping immediately after the bars come out of the oven. Cool, then cut into 2-inch squares.

To make the chocolate glaze, melt the semisweet and unsweetened chocolate in the top of a double boiler. Drizzle on the bars. Allow to set.

Carolyn Rosen, Nashville, Tennessee
The Old Farmer's Almanac *Recipe Contest, Dublin, New Hampshire*

Caramel Rocky Road Bars

2 dozen bars

When Kimberly Roland was 13. she entered this recipe in the junior division of cookies and won "Best of Show."

Crust

1 cup flour
¾ cup quick-cooking or old-fashioned oats
½ cup sugar
½ cup (1 stick) butter, softened
½ teaspoon baking soda
¼ teaspoon salt
¼ cup salted peanuts, chopped

Filling

½ cup caramel ice cream topping
½ cup salted peanuts
1½ cups miniature marshmallows
½ cup milk chocolate chips

To make the crust, preheat the oven to 350°F. Grease and flour a 9-inch square baking pan. In a small mixing bowl, combine the flour, oats, sugar, butter, baking soda, and salt. Beat on low, scraping the bowl often, until the mixture is crumbly, about 1 to 2 minutes. Stir in the peanuts. Reserve ¾ cup of this mixture. Press the remaining mixture into the prepared pan. Bake for 12 to 17 minutes, or until lightly browned. Maintain the oven temperature.

To make the filling, spread the caramel topping over the hot crust. Sprinkle the peanuts, marshmallows, and chocolate chips over the top. Sprinkle on the reserved crumb mixture. Bake for 20 to 25 minutes, or until lightly browned. Cover and refrigerate for 1 to 2 hours, or until firm. Cut into bars with a warm knife.

Kimberly Roland, Forney, Texas
State Fair of Texas, Dallas, Texas

Yam-Oatmeal Squares

2 dozen squares

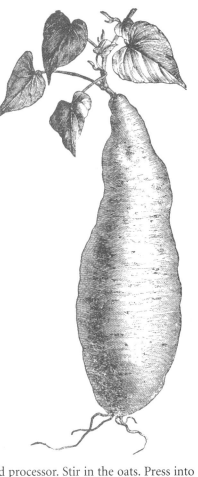

Crust

    2 cups flour
    1 cup brown sugar
    1 cup (2 sticks) butter or margarine
    1 cup quick-cooking oats

Filling

    3 cups mashed sweet potatoes (about
        2 large sweet potatoes)
    1 teaspoon ground cinnamon
    ½ teaspoon ground nutmeg
    1 teaspoon vanilla extract
    1 cup evaporated milk
    1 cup sugar
    2 eggs
    ½ teaspoon salt

Topping

    1 cup pecans, chopped
    ¼ cup (½ stick) butter or margarine
    1 cup brown sugar

To make the crust, preheat the oven to 350°F. Combine the flour and brown sugar. Cut in the butter using a pastry blender or food processor. Stir in the oats. Press into an ungreased 13x9-inch baking pan. Bake for 15 minutes. Maintain the oven temperature.

To make the filling, combine all the ingredients. Pour over the crust. Bake for 20 minutes. Maintain the oven temperature.

To make the topping, combine all the ingredients. Sprinkle over the filling. Bake for 15 to 20 minutes, or until set. Cool, then cut into squares.

Suzette Leonard, Tabor City, North Carolina
North Carolina Yam Festival, Tabor City, North Carolina

The World's Best Brownies

4 dozen brownies

6 squares (6 ounces) unsweetened chocolate
1 cup (2 sticks) butter or margarine
6 eggs
3 cups sugar
3 tablespoons vanilla extract
¾ cup milk
2 cups flour
1½ teaspoons salt
1½ cups walnuts, chopped

Preheat the oven to 350°F. Grease and flour a 15x10-inch jelly-roll pan. Melt the chocolate and butter in the top of a double boiler. Cool slightly. Beat the eggs until very thick, about 5 minutes. Gradually add the sugar and continue beating. Add the chocolate mixture and continue beating. Mix in the vanilla and milk and beat until smooth. Combine the flour and salt and add to the batter in fourths, beating well after each addition. Stir in the walnuts. Pour into the prepared pan and bake for 25 to 35 minutes, or until a toothpick inserted in the center comes out clean. Cool completely, then cut into bars.

Susan A. Silvashy, Laredo, Texas
Canfield Fair, Canfield, Ohio

Cherry-Filled White Chocolate Bars

20 bars

½ cup (1 stick) unsalted butter
1 package (12 ounces) white chocolate chips, divided
2 eggs
½ cup sugar
1 cup flour
½ teaspoon salt
½ teaspoon almond extract
½ cup sweetened coconut
½ cup cherry preserves
¼ cup sliced almonds

Preheat the oven to 325°F. Grease and flour an 8-inch square baking pan. Melt the butter in a small saucepan over low heat. Remove from the heat and add 1 cup of the white chocolate chips. Do not stir.

In a large bowl, beat the eggs until foamy. Add the sugar gradually, then stir in the chocolate mixture. Add the flour, salt, and almond extract. Mix just until blended. Spread half the mixture in the prepared pan. Bake for 15 to 20 minutes, or until light golden brown.

Meanwhile, add the remaining white chocolate chips and coconut to the remaining batter. Melt the cherry preserves over low heat. When the crust is ready, spread with the preserves and gently spoon the batter on top, spreading it to the edges. Sprinkle with the almonds. Bake for 20 to 25 minutes, or until set and light brown. Cool completely, then cut into bars.

Jackie de Matteis-O'Brien, Powell, Ohio
Ohio State Fair, Columbus, Ohio

Cream Cheese Swirl Brownies

9 large or 16 small brownies

Batter

> **4 squares (4 ounces) unsweetened chocolate**
> **½ cup (1 stick) butter**
> **1¼ cups sugar**
> **½ teaspoon vanilla extract**
> **3 eggs**
> **¾ cup flour**

Filling

> **1 package (8 ounces) cream cheese**
> **1½ teaspoons flour**
> **5 tablespoons sugar**
> **1 egg**
> **¼ teaspoon vanilla extract**

Preheat the oven to 350°F. Grease an 8-inch square cake pan.

To make the batter, melt the chocolate and butter over low heat. Cool for 5 minutes. With an electric mixer, beat together the chocolate mixture, sugar, and vanilla. Beat in the eggs one at a time. Blend in the flour. Set aside.

To make the filling, beat together the cream cheese, flour, sugar, egg, and vanilla.

Spread about two-thirds of the batter in the bottom of the pan. Gently spread the filling over the batter. Spoon the remaining batter over the filling. Bake for 50 minutes. Cool in the pan, then cut into squares.

Mary Michelli, Leesburg, Georgia
Georgia National Fair, Perry, Georgia

Chapter 9

Cookies

Cranberry-Coconut Cookies with Toffee

18 cookies

It's really hard to eat just one of these yummy little treats, which look just as nice as they taste.

Crusts

> ½ cup (1 stick) butter
> 1 package (3 ounces) cream cheese, softened
> 1 cup flour

Filling

> 1 tablespoon butter, softened
> 3 tablespoons brown sugar
> 1 tablespoon milk
> ½ cup sweetened coconut
> ½ cup fresh or frozen cranberries, coarsely chopped
> ½ cup crushed chocolate-coated English toffee bars (two 1.4-ounce bars)

To make the crusts, preheat the oven to 350°F. Beat the butter and cream cheese. Stir in the flour. (This also works well in a food processor.) Cover and chill for about 1 hour, or until easy to handle. Shape into 18 balls (1-inch). Press into the bottom and up the sides of 1¾-inch muffin cups (mini-muffins). Bake for 10 minutes.

To make the filling, cream the butter and brown sugar. Add the milk and stir until well mixed. Stir in the coconut, cranberries, and crushed toffee bars. Fill the crusts with the cranberry mixture. Bake for 10 minutes more. Let cool in the pan for at least 10 minutes before removing.

Ann Marie Briand, New Bedford, Massachusetts
Cranberry Harvest Festival, East Wareham, Massachusetts

Empire Biscuits

20 cookies

These "biscuits" won first place in the Scottish Faire contest, and it is no wonder: The cook is from Scotland and has served as treasurer of the Scottish Society of Iowa. She says that "everyone in Scotland makes this cookie." They are perfect for a formal tea but will be appreciated just as much in your child's lunch box.

2¼ cups flour
½ cup sugar
1 cup (2 sticks) butter, softened
Raspberry preserves
Confectioners' sugar

Preheat the oven to 325°F. Mix together the flour and sugar. Add the butter, working the dough together to form a ball. (This can be done in a food processor.) Turn out onto a lightly floured surface and roll out to a ⅛-inch thickness. Cut into 2-inch rounds. Place on ungreased cookie sheets and bake for 10 to 12 minutes. Cool on wire racks. When cool, sandwich 2 cookies together with raspberry preserves and sprinkle with confectioners' sugar.

Ann McWilliam, Melbourne, Iowa
Iowa State Fair, Des Moines, Iowa

Triple-Peanut Cookies

50 cookies

Peanut butter aficionados, take note! There's no shortage of real peanut flavor in these cute cookies.

- ½ cup granulated sugar
- ½ cup firmly packed brown sugar
- ½ cup shortening
- ¾ cup chunky peanut butter, divided
- 2 tablespoons light corn syrup
- 1 tablespoon milk
- ½ teaspoon vanilla extract
- 1½ cups flour
- ½ teaspoon baking soda
- ¼ teaspoon salt
- ½ cup roasted peanuts, chopped

Preheat the oven to 350°F. In a large bowl, cream the granulated sugar, brown sugar, shortening, and ½ cup of the peanut butter with an electric mixer. Blend in the corn syrup, milk, and vanilla. In a separate bowl, sift together the flour, baking soda, and salt. Add to the creamed mixture, mixing thoroughly. Shape into a 1½-inch roll approximately 18 inches long. Wrap in plastic wrap and chill for at least 2 hours.

Carefully cut the dough into ¼-inch slices. Place on ungreased cookie sheets and spread each cookie with a little of the reserved peanut butter. Crimp the edges with a fork and sprinkle the top with roasted peanuts. Bake for 12 to 14 minutes, or until lightly browned. (Do not overbake.) Cool on wire racks.

Shelly Ann Britton, Rochester, New Hampshire
Sandwich Fair, Center Sandwich, New Hampshire

Chocolate-Orange Delights

6 dozen cookies

The hint of orange adds just the right touch to these chocolaty goodies.

Cookies

    3 squares (3 ounces) unsweetened chocolate
    ¾ cup (1½ sticks) butter
    1 cup firmly packed brown sugar
    1 cup granulated sugar
    ½ cup sour cream
    2 eggs
    2 teaspoons grated orange rind
    2 cups flour
    1 teaspoon baking soda
    ½ teaspoon salt
    1 cup walnuts or pecans, chopped
    1 package (12 ounces) semisweet chocolate chips

Glaze

    3 squares (3 ounces) semisweet chocolate
    1 teaspoon orange extract
    4 tablespoons (½ stick) butter
    Candy sprinkles (optional)

To make the cookies, preheat the oven to 375°F. Melt the unsweetened chocolate and cool. Cream the butter, brown sugar, and granulated sugar until very light. Add the sour cream, eggs, orange rind, and melted chocolate; beat well. Stir in the flour, baking soda, and salt. Add the nuts and chocolate chips. Drop by rounded teaspoonfuls onto lightly greased cookie sheets. Bake for 12 to 15 minutes. Cool on wire racks.

To make the glaze, melt the chocolate with the orange extract in a small, heavy saucepan over low heat. Add the butter 1 tablespoon at a time. Stir until smooth. Spread on the cookies. If desired, decorate with candy sprinkles before the glaze hardens.

Frances E. Callahan, Chester, Vermont
The Old Farmer's Almanac *Recipe Contest, Dublin, New Hampshire*

Apple-Toffee Cookies

4 dozen cookies

For all those who love candied apples, these cookies combine caramel and apple in a form much easier to pack in a lunch box.

½ cup (1 stick) butter
½ cup shortening
1½ cups sugar
2 eggs
2¾ cups flour
2 teaspoons ground cinnamon
2 teaspoons cream of tartar
1 teaspoon baking soda
¾ teaspoon salt
1 package (8 ounces) almond brickle chips
1 cup dried apples, diced

Preheat the oven to 400°F. Beat the butter, shortening, sugar, and eggs together until thoroughly mixed. Sift together the flour, cinnamon, cream of tartar, baking soda, and salt. Stir into the butter mixture until well combined. Add the almond brickle chips and dried apples; mix well. Spoon the mixture by teaspoonfuls onto ungreased cookie sheets. Bake for 8 to 10 minutes, or until lightly browned. (Do not overbake. The cookies will not be set in the middle.) Cool on wire racks.

Joy White, Noblesville, Indiana
Indiana State Fair, Indianapolis, Indiana

BLUE RIBBON TIP

★ ★ ★ ★ ★

CHOPPING DRIED FRUIT

Dried fruit such as apples is very easy to chop using a meat grinder. Use the coarse blade and just run the fruit through. A food processor does not work well because the fruit can stick to the blade and become mushy.

Chocolate Peppermint Creams

3 dozen cookies

Consider these the cookie version of a peppermint patty. Our recipe tester notes, "My mother, who loves chocolate and peppermint, kept sneaking off to have another one of these. I was quite surprised, but this cookie seemed to bring out the 5-year-old in her."

Cookies

- 3 cups flour
- 1¼ teaspoons baking soda
- ½ teaspoon salt
- ¾ cup (1½ sticks) butter
- 1½ cups firmly packed brown sugar
- 2 tablespoons water
- 1 package (12 ounces) semisweet chocolate chips
- 2 eggs

Peppermint Cream

- 3 cups confectioners' sugar
- ⅓ cup butter, softened
- ¼ teaspoon peppermint extract (or to taste)
- ¼ cup milk

To make the cookies, preheat the oven to 350°F. Sift together the flour, baking soda, and salt. In a large saucepan over low heat, melt the butter with the brown sugar and water. Add the chocolate chips and stir to melt. Remove from the heat, cool slightly, and beat in the eggs. Add the flour mixture and mix well. Drop by heaping teaspoonfuls onto greased cookie sheets and bake for 8 to 10 minutes. Cool on wire racks.

To make the peppermint cream, blend all the ingredients with a mixer until smooth. Sandwich pairs of cookies together with 1 teaspoon peppermint cream. Cookies taste best a few days after baking and freeze beautifully.

Roselie A. Aiello, Mount Shasta, California
The Old Farmer's Almanac *Recipe Contest, Dublin, New Hampshire*

Sima's Yummy Rugelach

2 dozen cookies

Sima Firine's mother brought this recipe from Russia when the family was smuggled out of the country in 1922. By 1998, when the recipe was first published in this collection, Sima believed that she had made these cookies several hundred times. Their name means "little horns," and that's just what they look like. The cream cheese makes for a delicious pastry. Although Sima passed away in 2004 at the age of 95, her "yummy," hand-me-down recipe lives on.

½ cup (1 stick) unsalted butter, softened
1 package (8 ounces) cream cheese, softened
1 cup flour
½ cup walnuts, finely chopped
¼ cup sugar
½ teaspoon ground cinnamon

Cream the butter and cream cheese. Add the flour and mix well. (This can be done in a food processor.) Divide the dough in half and flatten. Wrap each half in wax paper and refrigerate overnight.

Preheat the oven to 350°F. Stir the walnuts, sugar, and cinnamon together in a small bowl. Roll out each half of the dough into an 8-inch circle. Sprinkle each with half the nut mixture. Cut each into 12 pie-shaped pieces. Starting at the wide end of each piece, roll it up toward the point. Place on a greased cookie sheet and bake for 20 minutes.

Sima Firine, Poughkeepsie, New York
Dutchess County Fair, Rhinebeck, New York

Molasses Cookies

5 dozen cookies

1½ cups shortening
2 cups sugar
½ cup light molasses
2 eggs
4 cups flour
4 teaspoons baking soda
1 teaspoon salt
1 teaspoon ground cloves
1 teaspoon ground ginger
2 heaping teaspoons ground
   cinnamon
Sugar for rolling

Preheat the oven to 375°F. Cream the shortening and sugar. Add the molasses and eggs and beat. Add the flour, baking soda, salt, cloves, ginger, and cinnamon. Beat until well blended. Chill for 10 minutes. Roll into 1-inch balls. Roll in sugar, covering the balls completely. Bake on ungreased cookie sheets for 8 to 10 minutes. Cool on wire racks.

Kathy Mintun, San Francisco, California
California Exposition and State Fair,
Sacramento, California

BLUE RIBBON TIP

★ ★ ★ ★ ★

CINNAMON

Cinnamon is one of the most flavorful and best-known spices in the world. It is cultivated in Indonesia, China, Vietnam, and Sri Lanka (formerly Ceylon). Korintje Cassia cinnamon grows wild on the southern coast of Sumatra and is preferred by many bakers for its smooth flavor with less bite. Chinese cinnamon is stronger and spicier and has only recently become available outside China. Vietnamese cinnamon is the strongest cinnamon and is extremely sweet and flavorful. Ceylonese cinnamon, also known as true cinnamon, is unfamiliar to most Americans. It is not as strong as the other types, but it is preferred in England and Mexico.

German Hazelnut Cookies

5 dozen cookies

These are an authentic Old World Christmas treat, but we recommend that you don't save them just for Christmas!

- 3 cups flour
- 3 cups (6 sticks) ice-cold unsalted butter
- 3 cups confectioners' sugar
- 3½ cups ground hazelnuts or walnuts, divided
- 3 eggs, well beaten
- Juice and grated rind of 1 lemon
- 1 egg beaten with 1 tablespoon water

Measure the flour into a large bowl and cut in the butter. (This can be done in batches in a food processor.) Stir in the confectioners' sugar and 3 cups of the nuts. Add the eggs and lemon juice and rind. Cover tightly with plastic wrap and chill thoroughly, at least 2 hours.

Preheat the oven to 350°F. Working with a small amount of dough at a time (keep the rest of the dough refrigerated), roll out to a ¼-inch thickness on a floured surface. Cut with cookie cutters and transfer to greased cookie sheets. (The dough also may be dropped by teaspoonfuls. The cookies will flatten into brown-edged wafers as they bake.) Brush gently with the egg-water mixture and sprinkle with the remaining nuts. Bake until golden, 10 to 15 minutes.

Betty P. Race, Euclid, Ohio
The Old Farmer's Almanac *Recipe Contest,*
Dublin, New Hampshire

Triple-Treat Peanut Butter Chocolate Chip Cookies

4 to 5 dozen cookies

These cookies make an ideal lunch box treat. Chocolate chips, oats, and peanut butter in one delicious cookie: Who says you can't have it all?

1½ cups old-fashioned oats, divided
2 cups flour
1 teaspoon baking powder
1 teaspoon baking soda
1 teaspoon salt
1 cup (2 sticks) unsalted butter, softened
1 cup granulated sugar
1 cup firmly packed light-brown sugar
1 tablespoon vanilla extract
¾ cup creamy peanut butter
2 eggs
1 package (12 ounces) semisweet chocolate chips
Reese's Pieces

Grind 1 cup of the oats in a blender or food processor until fine. In a large bowl, stir together the ground oats, remaining ½ cup whole oats, flour, baking powder, baking soda, and salt. In another bowl, cream the butter, granulated sugar, and brown sugar until light and fluffy. Beat in the vanilla and peanut butter. Beat in the eggs one at a time. Gradually add the oatmeal mixture and mix well. Stir in the chocolate chips. Chill for at least 2 hours (up to 1 week).

Preheat the oven to 325°F. Roll the dough into balls about 1 to 2 inches in diameter. Press a Reese's Piece on top of each one and place on an ungreased cookie sheet. Bake for 11 to 14 minutes. The cookies will be just barely set. Cool on wire racks.

Robin L. Warchol, Clinton Township, Michigan
Michigan State Fair, Detroit, Michigan

Raspberry-Orange Mazurkas

32 pastries

The mazurka is a traditional Polish dance. These heirloom Polish goodies are just as pretty and have the same exotic appeal as the spirited dance.

Crust

> 1 cup (2 sticks) unsalted butter, softened
> 1½ cups flour
> 1¼ cups confectioners' sugar
> ½ teaspoon salt
> 6 egg yolks
> 2 teaspoons orange extract
> 1 cup pecans, finely chopped

Topping

> 1 cup raspberry preserves
> 2 tablespoons orange liqueur
> 1 tablespoon grated orange rind

To make the crust, preheat the oven to 325°F. Grease and flour two 9- or 10-inch round cake pans. Cream the butter until light. Combine the flour, confectioners' sugar, and salt. Add to the butter alternately with the egg yolks. Add the orange extract and beat until smooth. Fold in the pecans. Pat into the prepared pans and bake for 35 to 40 minutes, or until golden. Cool on wire racks.

To make the topping, heat all the ingredients in a small saucepan. Strain the warm topping through a fine sieve. Using a serrated knife, cut each mazurka into 16 wedges, place on a serving tray, and glaze with the topping.

Kathy Lee, Valley Center, California
The Old Farmer's Almanac *Recipe Contest, Dublin, New Hampshire*

White Chip Chocolate Cookies

5 dozen cookies

Here are some chocolate chip cookies in reverse—white chocolate chips in a dark chocolate cookie.

- **1 cup (2 sticks) butter**
- **¾ cup granulated sugar**
- **⅔ cup brown sugar**
- **2 eggs**
- **1 teaspoon vanilla extract**
- **2¼ cups flour**
- **¾ cup unsweetened cocoa**
- **1 teaspoon baking soda**
- **½ teaspoon salt**
- **1 package (12 ounces) white chocolate chips**

Preheat the oven to 350°F. Beat the butter, granulated sugar, and brown sugar until fluffy. Beat in the eggs and vanilla. Sift together the flour, cocoa, baking soda, and salt. Beat into the batter until well mixed. Stir in the white chocolate chips. Drop by tablespoonfuls onto ungreased cookie sheets. Bake for 9 to 11 minutes. (Do not overbake.) Remove from the sheets immediately and cool on wire racks.

Jennifer Davis, Wellington, Kansas
Kansas Wheat Festival, Wellington, Kansas

Grandma's Best Butter Cookies

4 dozen cookies

This truly versatile recipe works just as well whether you make cookie-cutter cookies, cookies molded in a cookie press, refrigerator cookies, or just plain drop cookies. And no one can eat just one! Every cook needs this recipe in his or her repertoire.

1 cup (2 sticks) butter, softened
¾ cup sugar
2 egg yolks
1 teaspoon vanilla extract, or 1½ teaspoons almond extract
2¼ cups flour
¼ teaspoon salt

Cream the butter and sugar until light and fluffy. Add the egg yolks and vanilla or almond extract and beat well. Sift the flour and salt into the batter and beat until well mixed.

To make drop cookies, preheat the oven to 350°F. Drop unchilled dough by teaspoonfuls onto cookie sheets lined with parchment paper (or ungreased). Bake for about 10 minutes, or until just barely brown at the edges. Cool on wire racks.

To make rolled (refrigerator) cookies, shape the dough into 2 rolls, each 1½ inches in diameter. Wrap in wax paper and chill for at least 1 hour. Preheat the oven to 350°F. If you wish, roll the dough in colored sugar, chocolate sprinkles, or rainbow sprinkles. Cut each roll into ½-inch slices, place on cookie sheets lined with parchment paper, and bake for 10 minutes. (Do not brown.) Cool on wire racks and store in an airtight container.

To make cookie-cutter cookies, chill the dough. Preheat the oven to 350°F. Roll out the dough between floured wax paper to a ½-inch thickness. Cut with cookie cutters (small ones work best). Place on parchment-lined cookie sheets and bake for 10 minutes. Cool on wire racks and decorate if desired. Sandwich cookies may be made by sticking two cookies together with preserves or almond filling.

To make molded cookies, preheat the oven to 350°F. Put the unchilled dough in a pastry bag with a big star tip or in a cookie press fitted with a design plate. Drop the cookies onto parchment-lined cookie sheets and bake for 10 minutes. Cool on wire racks. (Our recipe tester notes, "The molded cookies worked about the most easily in the cookie press of any recipe I have tried.")

Mary Ann Saint, Plymouth, Michigan
Michigan State Fair, Detroit, Michigan

BLUE RIBBON TIP

★ ★ ★ ★ ★

DON'T DISCARD THOSE EGG WHITES!

Egg whites can be stored in the refrigerator or freezer. Keep an airtight container in the refrigerator for them. When a recipe calls for yolks, simply save the leftover whites in this container, where they will keep quite well for at least a month. When enough have accumulated, you can make an angel food cake. In the meantime, there are always enough to provide a few extra for a recipe or to add to a meringue for a pie, making it extra high.

Orange Citrus Cookies

2 dozen cookies

Cookies

½ cup (1 stick) butter
1 cup sugar
1 egg
½ cup sour milk, or ½ cup milk plus ½ teaspoon lemon juice
3 cups flour
½ teaspoon baking soda
1 teaspoon baking powder
1 teaspoon orange extract
2 teaspoons grated orange rind
⅓ cup orange juice

Icing

3 tablespoons butter, softened
½ to 1 cup confectioners' sugar
1 drop red food coloring
1 drop yellow food coloring

To make the cookies, preheat the oven to 375°F. Cream the butter and sugar. Add the egg and beat well. Stir in the milk. Combine the flour, baking soda, and baking powder and add to the sugar mixture. Add the orange extract, orange rind, and orange juice and mix well. Drop by large spoonfuls on lightly greased cookie sheets. Bake for 10 to 12 minutes, or until just barely browned. Cool on wire racks.

To make the icing, cream the butter. Add enough confectioners' sugar to make the icing of spreading consistency. Add the red and yellow food coloring, then spread on the cooled cookies.

Jan Herrmann-Beach, Mesa, Arizona
Arizona State Fair, Phoenix, Arizona

For more recipes and kitchen tips, go to Almanac.com/food.

Cherry Thumbprints

About 2 dozen cookies

½ cup blanched whole almonds
¾ cup sugar
¾ cup (1½ sticks) unsalted butter, at room temperature
1 large egg, at room temperature
1 teaspoon vanilla extract
½ teaspoon almond extract
2 cups unbleached, all-purpose flour
½ teaspoon baking powder
½ teaspoon salt
1 small jar cherry preserves

Put the almonds and sugar into the bowl of a food processor and process nuts to a fine meal. Transfer to a small bowl. Cream the butter with an electric mixer, gradually adding the almond mixture. Beat in the egg until the mixture is light, then add the vanilla and almond extracts. Mix the flour, baking powder, and salt in a separate bowl, stirring it into the creamed mixture in several stages. Cover the dough and refrigerate for 15 minutes.

Preheat the oven to 350°F. Pinch off pieces of dough and roll them into 1¼-inch balls. Place the balls onto ungreased cookie sheets, pressing a thumb deeply into the center of the dough to make a large crater. Leave about 2 inches between each cookie. Mound the craters with cherry preserves and bake the cookies for 15 to 20 minutes, until the bottom edge of the cookie just begins to brown. Cool briefly on sheets, then transfer to a rack to finish cooling.

Zucchini Drop Cookies

3 dozen cookies

1 cup grated zucchini
1 teaspoon baking soda
1 cup sugar
½ cup (1 stick) shortening or butter
1 egg, beaten
2 cups flour
1 teaspoon cinnamon
½ teaspoon ground cloves
½ teaspoon salt
1 cup chopped nuts
1 cup raisins

Preheat the oven to 375°F. Mix together zucchini, baking soda, sugar, butter, and beaten egg. Sift in flour, cinnamon, cloves, and salt. Stir to blend. Stir in nuts and raisins, and drop batter by the teaspoonful onto a greased cookie sheet. Bake 12 to 15 minutes. Cool on a wire rack.

Chapter 10

Too Good to
Leave Out

Blueberry Bread Pudding

6 to 8 servings

1 quart fresh or frozen blueberries, preferably wild
¾ to 1 cup sugar
1 piece cinnamon stick and/or 1 twist fresh lemon peel
1 small loaf homemade or Pepperidge Farm–type white bread, slightly stale,
    crusts removed
1 pint heavy cream
1 teaspoon sugar

In a large saucepan, cook the berries with sugar, water to barely cover, and cinnamon stick and/or lemon peel over low heat until the berries have burst and the mixture is syrupy, about 15 minutes. Remove from heat.

To build a bread pudding in a deep, round dish: Cover the bottom of the dish with a layer of bread, cut into irregular pieces to fit the dish; then spoon on the liquid and berries until the bread is soaked and purple. Add another layer of bread; douse it with berries, and so on, until the dish is filled. Pour the last of the liquid over the top and refrigerate with a weighted dish on top.

Before serving, whip the cream, sweeten it with the sugar, and cover the pudding with a thick layer. The pudding can be molded for a prettier look and inverted onto a plate. Coat the pudding with the whipped cream.

Apple Dumplings

4 servings

Dumpling Dough

- 1¾ cups flour
- ¾ teaspoon salt
- 3 teaspoons baking powder
- 1 tablespoon sugar
- 6 tablespoons chilled butter or shortening
- ¾ cup milk

Apples

- ¾ cup brown sugar
- ¼ cup (½ stick) butter, softened
- ¼ teaspoon salt
- ½ teaspoon cinnamon
- 4 medium apples, peeled and cored
- 1 egg white

Preheat the oven to 450°F.

For dumplings: Mix together flour, salt, baking powder, and sugar. Cut solid shortening into dry ingredients, make a well in the center, and add milk. Stir just until dough is fairly free from sides of bowl. Turn onto lightly floured board and knead 8 to 10 times. Cover and chill while preparing apples.

For apples: Combine sugar, butter, salt, and cinnamon and fill apple core hollows with this mixture, reserving some to sprinkle on top. Roll out dough to ¼-inch thick and cut into 4 squares. Place an apple onto each square and spread remaining sugar mixture over apples. Bring up corners of dough to cover apple and press edges together (dampen with a little water if necessary). Make sure edges are sealed, or dumplings will pop open during baking. Brush with egg white and prick tops of dumplings with a fork. Carefully transfer dumplings to a baking pan. Bake for 10 minutes, then reduce heat to 350°F and continue baking for about 40 minutes longer, or until apples are tender when tested with a toothpick. Serve with cream.

German Apple Pancakes

6 servings

5 eggs
1¾ cups milk
¼ cup (½ stick) butter, melted
1½ cups flour
⅓ cup sugar
¾ teaspoon salt
Extra melted butter, to brush pan and top of cooked pancakes
4 apples, peeled, cored, and sliced thin
Cinnamon and sugar
Extra unmelted butter, to dot pancakes while cooking

Preheat the oven to 400°F. In a bowl, beat the eggs and milk. Add the melted butter, flour, sugar, and salt, and blend until smooth. Heat a 10-inch ovenproof skillet, and brush with butter. Pour ¾ cup of batter evenly into pan. When pancake is set, cover with a layer of apples. Sprinkle with cinnamon and sugar, and dot with butter.

Bake for 3 minutes. Fold pancake so apples are inside. Remove to a plate. Brush top with butter, and sprinkle with additional cinnamon and sugar. After all six pancakes are done, arrange on an ovenproof platter, and brown under the broiler. Serve at once.

For more recipes and kitchen tips, go to Almanac.com/food.

Zucchini Pizza

8 servings

Crust

> 3 to 4 cups coarsely grated zucchini (use a hand grater
>   or a food processor)
> 1 teaspoon salt
> 2 eggs, beaten
> ⅓ cup flour
> ½ cup grated mozzarella or cheddar cheese
> ½ cup grated Parmesan or Romano cheese
> 2 tablespoons fresh basil, or 1 teaspoon dried
> Salt and freshly ground black pepper, to taste

Topping

> ¼ to ½ cup tomato sauce
> Choice of sautéed mushrooms or peppers, sliced cooked sausage,
>   fresh tomatoes, olives, etc.
> ½ to 1 cup grated cheese (your favorite kind)

For crust: Sprinkle the grated zucchini with salt, toss, and let sit in a colander for 30 minutes. Squeeze out excess moisture with your hands.

Preheat the oven to 350°F. In a large mixing bowl, combine the zucchini, eggs, flour, cheeses, and basil and season with salt and pepper. Spread mixture into a lightly oiled 10-inch round or 13x9-inch baking pan. Bake 20 to 25 minutes, or until the surface is dry and just beginning to brown. Broil for 5 minutes, until top is firm and lightly browned. Remove from oven.

For topping: Spread tomato sauce over crust. Arrange your favorite toppings over the sauce and sprinkle with cheese. Bake at 350°F for another 10 to 15 minutes, or until cheese is melted and bubbling.

Gougères

3 dozen

5 tablespoons butter
1 teaspoon salt
¼ teaspoon freshly ground black pepper
¼ teaspoon freshly ground nutmeg
1 cup plus ½ tablespoon water
1 cup all-purpose flour
1 cup grated Gruyère cheese
5 large eggs at room temperature (very important)

Preheat the oven to 425°F. In a medium saucepan, combine the butter, salt, pepper, nutmeg, and 1 cup water. Bring to a boil over medium-high heat. When the butter melts, reduce the heat to low. Add the flour to the butter water mixture all at once, and cook over low heat, beating with a wooden spoon for 1 to 2 minutes, until the mixture pulls away from the sides of the pan. Remove pan from heat. Add the cheese and beat with the wooden spoon until well incorporated. Add 4 of the eggs, 1 at a time, beating each egg into the batter with the wooden spoon until thoroughly absorbed. Continue beating the mixture until it is smooth, shiny, and firm.

Drop the batter by small spoonfuls onto a lightly greased cookie sheet. Beat the remaining egg with ½ tablespoon water, then brush it onto the tops of the uncooked gougères. Bake in the upper third of the oven for 15 to 20 minutes, or until golden and doubled in size. Remove from the oven and serve hot, or allow to cool to room temperature.

Blueberry Oatmeal Crisp

8 to 10 servings

Fruit

>   3 pints blueberries
>   ½ cup sugar
>   Juice and finely grated zest of 1 lemon
>   3 tablespoons flour

Topping

>   1 cup unbleached all-purpose flour
>   1 cup packed light-brown sugar
>   ⅔ cup rolled oats
>   ½ teaspoon cinnamon
>   ¼ teaspoon salt
>   ½ cup (1 stick) plus 2 tablespoons cold, unsalted butter,
>   cut into small pieces

Mix the berries, sugar, lemon juice and zest, and flour in a large bowl. Preheat the oven to 400°F, and butter a 13x9-inch glass or ceramic baking dish.

For topping: Combine the flour, brown sugar, oats, cinnamon, and salt in the bowl of a food processor. Add the butter, and pulse the machine repeatedly, in 2- to 3-second bursts, until the mixture is clumpy, like damp crumbs. Transfer the berries to the baking dish, and spread the crumbs evenly over the fruit. Bake for 30 minutes, until bubbly hot. Serve at any temperature, although it is best to let it cool at least 10 minutes.

Cream of Tartar Biscuits

8 to 12 biscuits

2 cups flour
4 teaspoons cream of tartar
1 teaspoon baking soda
½ teaspoon salt
¼ cup lard
¾ cup cold milk
Butter, to top

Preheat the oven to 475°F. Sift flour, cream of tartar, baking soda, and salt into a medium bowl. Cut in lard using a pastry blender. Add milk all at once and toss with fork. Knead 5 or 6 times on a lightly floured board, and roll or pat to a ½- or ¾-inch thickness. Cut with a biscuit cutter, and top each biscuit with a bit of butter. Place onto a greased cookie sheet and bake for 5 minutes. Turn off heat and leave in the oven for 5 to 10 minutes longer, until golden. Serve hot.

For more recipes and kitchen tips, go to Almanac.com/food.

Appendix

List of Fairs, Festivals & Bake-offs

Please contact organizers at the addresses and telephone numbers below for dates of fairs and guidelines for submitting entries. Also, please verify the cost of cookbooks and shipping fees before placing orders.

ALABAMA

National Peanut Festival
5622 Hwy. 231 South
Dothan, AL 36301
(334) 793-4323
For a brochure of winning recipes, send a self-addressed, stamped envelope to the address above.

ARIZONA

Arizona State Fair
1826 W. McDowell Rd.
Phoenix, AZ 85005
(602) 252-6771

CALIFORNIA

National Date Festival
Fairgrounds Office
46-350 Arabia St.
Indio, CA 92201
(800) 811-3247

California Exposition and State Fair
1600 Exposition Blvd.
Sacramento, CA 95815
(916) 263-3000 or (877) 225-3976

COLORADO

Colorado State Fair
100 Beulah Ave.
Pueblo, CO 81004
(719) 561-8484 or (800) 876-4567

DELAWARE

Delaware State Fair
South Dupont Hwy.
P.O. Box 28
Harrington, DE 19952
(302) 398-3269

GEORGIA

Georgia National Fair
401 Larry Walker Pkwy.
P.O. Box 1367
Perry, GA 31069
(478) 987-3247 or (800) 987-3247

ILLINOIS

National Pie Championship
American Pie Council
P.O. Box 368
Lake Forest, IL 60045
(847) 371-0170

Morton Pumpkin Festival
Morton Chamber of Commerce
415 W. Jefferson St.
Morton, IL 61550
(309) 263-2491 or (888) 765-6588

INDIANA
Indiana State Fair
1202 E. 38th St.
Indianapolis, IN 46205
(317) 927-7500

IOWA
Iowa State Fair
P.O. Box 57130
Des Moines, IA 50317-0003
(515) 262-3111

KANSAS
Wheat Festival
Wellington Area Chamber of Commerce
207 S. Washington St.
Wellington, KS 67152
(620) 326-7466

LOUISIANA
Louisiana Pecan Festival
P.O. Box 78
Colfax, LA 71417
(318) 627-5196

MAINE
Fryeburg Fair
P.O. Box 78
Fryeburg, ME 04037
(207) 935-3268

Machias Wild Blueberry Festival
Centre Street Congregational Church
P.O. Box 265
Machias, ME 04654
(207) 255-6665

Central Maine Egg Festival
P.O. Box 82
Pittsfield, ME 04969
(207) 257-4209

MASSACHUSETTS
Cranberry Harvest Festival
Cape Cod Cranberry Growers' Association
3203 B Cranberry Hwy.
East Wareham, MA 02538
(508) 759-1041

Franklin County Fair
89 Wisdom Way
P.O. Box 564
Greenfield, MA 01302
(413) 774-4282

Shelburne Grange Fair
P.O. Box 328
Shelburne, MA 01370
(413) 625-9924

MICHIGAN
Michigan State Fair
Exposition Center
1120 W. State Fair Ave.
Detroit, MI 48203
(313) 369-8250

National Cherry Festival
109 Sixth St.
Traverse City, MI 49684
(231) 947-4230

MINNESOTA

Minnesota State Fair
1265 Snelling Ave. North
St. Paul, MN 55108-3099
(651) 288-4400

MISSOURI

Ozark Empire Fair
3001 N. Grant
Springfield, MO 65803
(417) 833-2660

NEW HAMPSHIRE

Sandwich Fair
P.O. Box 161
Center Sandwich, NH 03227
(603) 284-7062

The Old Farmer's Almanac
Recipe Contest
P.O. Box 520
Dublin, NH 03444
(603) 563-8111
    Each year, the Almanac announces a contest that calls for recipes using a specific ingredient (chicken, apples, or eggs, for example). Cash prizes are awarded for the best original recipes submitted.

Great Gourd Bake-off
Pumpkin Festival
Center Stage Cheshire County
95 Main St.
Keene, NH 03431
(603) 358-5344

NEW JERSEY

Hunterdon County 4-H and
Agricultural Fair
P.O. Box 2900
Flemington, NJ 08551
(908) 782-6809

NEW YORK

Dutchess Agricultural Society
Dutchess County Fair
P.O. Box 389
Rhinebeck, NY 12572
(845) 876-4001

NORTH CAROLINA

North Carolina Yam Festival
P.O. Box 446
Tabor City, NC 28463
(910) 653-2031

OHIO

Canfield Fair
P.O. Box 250
Canfield, OH 44406
(330) 533-4107

Ohio State Fair
717 E. 17th Ave.
Columbus, OH 43211
(614) 644-3247

OKLAHOMA

Oklahoma State Fair
P.O. Box 74943
Oklahoma City, OK 73147
(405) 948-6700

OREGON

Oregon State Fair and Expo
2330 17th St. NE
Salem, OR 97303
(503) 947-3247

Springfield Filbert Festival
P.O. Box 480
Springfield, OR 97477
(541) 746-6750

RHODE ISLAND

Washington County Fair
841 A Moorsfield Rd.
Saunderstown, RI 02874
(401) 782-8139

TENNESSEE

Appalachian Fair
Appalachian Fair Association, Inc.
P.O. Box 8218
Gray, TN 37615
(423) 477-3211

TEXAS

Peach Jamboree and Rodeo
Stonewall Chamber of Commerce
P.O. Box 1
Stonewall, TX 78671
(830) 644-2735

State Fair of Texas
P.O. Box 150009
Dallas, TX 75315
(214) 565-9931

VERMONT

Vermont Dairy Festival
P.O. Box 34
Sheldon, VT 05483
(802) 933-4636

Champlain Valley Fair and Exposition
P.O. Box 209
Essex Junction, VT 05453
(802) 878-5545

VIRGINIA

Salem Fair
P.O. Box 886
Salem, VA 24153
(540) 375-3004

WASHINGTON

Western Washington Fair
P.O. Box 430
Puyallup, WA 98371
(253) 841-5045

WISCONSIN

Wisconsin State Fair
P.O. Box 14990
640 S. 84th St.
West Allis, WI 53214
(414) 266-7000

For more recipes and kitchen tips, go to Almanac.com/food.

Index

All-American Apple Pie, 124
Angel Food Cake, 104
Angie's Apple Crumb Pie, 120
anise
    Greek Anise Bread, 24
apple(s)
    All-American Apple Pie, 124
    Angie's Apple Crumb Pie, 120
    Apple Dumplings, 175
    Apple-Toffee Cookies, 160
    Apple-Walnut Celebration Cake, 87
    Apple-Walnut Poppy Seed Coffeecake, 52
    Bavarian Coffeecake, 58
    Blue Ribbon Tip, 114
    German Apple Pancakes, 176
    Great American Apple Pie, A, 115
apricot(s)
    Apricot-Almond Bars, 149
    Apricot Tea Ring, 56

Banana(s)
    Banana Bread, Great-Grandmother's, 45
    Banana Marble Pound Cake, 106
    Banana Nut Bread, 44
    Coconut-Banana Cream Pie, 130
Bars & Brownies, 143
    Apricot-Almond Bars, 149
    Caramel Rocky Road Bars, 150
    Cherry-Filled White Chocolate Bars, 153
    Cream Cheese Swirl Brownies, 154
    Decadent Brownies, 148
    Lemony Hazelnut Bars, 145
    Peanut Butter Bars, 147
    Pumpkin Cheesecake Bars, 144
    Triple-Good Bars, 146
    Yam-Oatmeal Squares, 151
    World's Best Brownies, The, 152
Bavarian Coffeecake, 58
Biscuits, Cream of Tartar, 180
Black Walnut Layer Cake, 80

blueberry(ies)
    Blueberry Bread Pudding, 174
    Blueberry Oatmeal Crisp, 179
    Blueberry Streusel Pie, 116
    Blue Ribbon Tip, 117
    Downeast Burgundy Berry Pie, 122
    Wild Blueberry Pie, 117
Blue Ribbon Tips
    baking, 18, 40
    creaming, 93
    eggs, 105, 169
    flours, 22, 29, 64, 70
    freezing, 50, 57
    fruits, 95, 101, 114, 117, 160
    nuts, 73, 79, 81, 99
    pan sizes, 60
    serving, 69
    spices, 39, 77, 119, 163
bran
    Date Bran Muffins, 40
Breads. *See* **Quick Breads & Muffins; Yeast Breads & Rolls**
Bread Pudding, Blueberry, 174
Brownies. *See* **Bars & Brownies**
Buttermilk Cake, Quick, 110
Buttermilk Poppy Seed Cake, 96
butterscotch
    Pumpkin-Butterscotch Mousse Pie, 132

Cakes. *See* Coffeecakes; Frosted Cakes; Unfrosted Cakes
caramel(s)
    Caramel Rocky Road Bars, 150
    Chocolate Caramel-Pecan Cheesecake, 103
    Nany's Caramel-Peanut Butter Cake, 74
caraway
    Sourdough Onion-Potato Rye Bread with Caraway, 26
Carrot Cake, The Best, Ever, 85

cheese(s)
  Cheddar Cheese Pepper Bread, 39
  Cheesecake, The World's Best, 112
  Chocolate Caramel-Pecan Cheesecake, 103
  Cream Cheese Cake, 63
  Cream Cheese Swirl Brownies, 154
  Orange Nut Bread with Orange Cream Cheese Spread, 43
  Pineapple Cheesecake, 102
  Pumpkin Cheesecake Bars, 144
  Sima's Yummy Rugelach, 162
  World's Best Cheesecake, The, 112
cherry(ies)
  Cherry-Filled White Chocolate Bars, 153
  Cherry Pie, 126
  Cherry Pudding Cake, 107
  Cherry Thumbprints, 171
  Michigan Cherry Muffins, 41
chocolate
  Banana Marble Pound Cake, 106
  Blue Ribbon Tip, 77
  Cherry-Filled White Chocolate Bars, 153
  Chocolate Birthday Cake, The Best, 88
  Chocolate Caramel-Pecan Cheesecake, 103
  Chocolate Coconut Cream Cake, 82
  Chocolate-Orange Delights, 159
  Chocolate Peppermint Creams, 161
  Chocolate-Rum Chiffon Pie, 134
  Chocolate Torte with Vanilla Sauce and Raspberries, 68
  Coffee Cream Pie with Chocolate Crust, 136
  Cream Cheese Swirl Brownies, 154
  Decadent Brownies, 148
  Moist Chocolate Cake with Cocoa Butter Frosting, 65
  Peanut Butter Chocolate Chip Cupcakes, 66
  Swiss Chocolate Cake, 72
  Triple-Treat Peanut Butter Chocolate Chip Cookies, 165
  White Chip Chocolate Cookies, 167
  World's Best Brownies, The, 152
Cinnamon Rolls, 33
coconut(s)
  Blue Ribbon Tip, 79
  Chocolate Coconut Cream Cake, 82
  Coconut-Banana Cream Pie, 130
  Coconut Cake, 92
  Cranberry-Coconut Cookies with Toffee, 156
  White Cake with Coconut and Whipped Cream, 78
coffee
  Coffee Cream Pie with Chocolate Crust, 136
Coffeecakes, 49
  Apple-Walnut Poppy Seed Coffeecake, 52
  Apricot Tea Ring, 56
  Bavarian Coffeecake, 58
  Coffeecake Muffins, 55
  Danish Nut Loaf, 50
  Orange Bowknot Rolls, 54
  Sour Cream Coffeecake #1, 53
  Sour Cream Coffeecake #2, 59
Cookies, 155
  Apple-Toffee Cookies, 160
  Cherry Thumbprints, 171
  Chocolate-Orange Delights, 159
  Chocolate Peppermint Creams, 161
  Cranberry-Coconut Cookies with Toffee, 156
  Empire Biscuits, 157
  German Hazelnut Cookies, 164
  Grandma's Best Butter Cookies, 168
  Molasses Cookies, 163
  Orange Citrus Cookies, 170
  Raspberry-Orange Mazurkas, 166
  Sima's Yummy Rugelach, 162
  Triple-Peanut Cookies, 158
  Triple-Treat Peanut Butter Chocolate Chip Cookies, 165
  White Chip Chocolate Cookies, 167
  Zucchini Drop Cookies, 172
Cooks
  Aiello, Roselie A., 161

Alimi, Sue, 117
Anderson, Jill, 148
Bequeath, Yolanda, 118
Bouchard, Melissa, 38
Briand, Ann Marie, 156
Britton, Shelly Ann, 158
Brook, Amber, 19
Burlew, Margaret, 133
Callahan, Frances E., 159
Casity, Shirley M., 135
Cole, Signe, 102
Cravens, Mrs. Howard, 121
Crossan, Sally, 106
Cummings, Mary, 137
Daniel, Melba, 130
Davis, Annie, 78
Davis, Jennifer, 167
Dayton, Loleta, 116
de Matteis-O'Brien, Jackie, 153
DeMatteo, Julie, 52
Dillon, Dorothy, 40
Donnelly, Reverend Nancy S., 16
Drake, Ashlene, 98
Ferris, Diana, 36
Firine, Sima, 162
Fish, Sharon, 147
Frajkar, Georgeann, 39
Fuqua, Amy, 115
Garey, Hilda, 96
Gaysek, Karin, 58
Giordano, Robin, 41
Haedrich, Ken, 100
Harlow, Connie, 140
Harter, Helen L., 62
Herrmann-Beach, Jan, 170
Hoenke, Mrs. Guy, 107
Hollis, Mrs. Cloyce, 20
Hurayt, Fran, 51
James, Emily, 99
Janas, Elaine, 30, 56
Janas-Johnson, Renee, 82
Johnson, Marjorie, 54
Johnson, Nancy, 80
Jordan, Persis, 122

Koski, Lilly R., 71
Laabs, Robin, 63
Lamp, Darlene R., 125
Leach, Stephanie, 25
Lee, Kathy, 166
Lemlin, Jeanne, 136
Leonard, Suzette, 151
Marble, Deedy, 43
Markey, Robert, 94
Martin, Theresa S., 76
McDowell, Nancy, 67
McWilliam, Ann, 12, 157
Medlin, Vickie, 22
Michelli, Mary, 154
Mintun, Kathy, 163
Moreton, Carolyn, 65, 146
Neavoll, Florence, 123
Neumayer, Marilyn, 68
Nichols. Sharon, 42
Osterman, Paul C., 26
O'Sullivan, Carrie, 92
Oxley, David, 28, 126
Price, Angie H., 120
Primeau, Nicole, 72
Race, Betty P., 164
Rassi, Paula, 132
Reiss, Tammy, 44, 84
Ritchie, Karen, 108
Roland, Kimberly, 150
Rosen, Carolyn, 149
Rovner, Kate Stewart, 134
Saint, Mary Ann, 168
Scheetz, Mary Frances, 21, 24
Schmaltz, Mary, 53
Shangraw, Kathleen, 32
Silvashy, Susan A., 152
Smith, Anne, 55
Smith, Susan, 104
Spitler, Terri, 74
St. Louis, Derolyn, 131
Stark, Cathy, 17
Steponaitis, Victoria, 37
Stocks, Raven, 138
Taylor, Deborah, 144

Cooks (continued)
Thomas, Jean, 124
Thomas, Kate, 12, 66, 139
Thomas, Sue, 31, 97
Warchol, Robin L., 103, 165
West, Ellen, 145
White, Joy, 160
Young, Susan, 95
Corn Bread, Skillet, 47
cornmeal
Cornmeal Yeast Rolls, 19
Cowboy Cobbler, 95
cranberry(ies)
Cranberry and Pear Butter Crumb Cake,
100
Cranberry-Coconut Cookies with Toffee,
156
Cranberry-Ginger Bread, 37
Cranberry-Orange Scones, 36
Cranberry Pie, 127
Cranberry-Walnut Chess Pie, 131
Downeast Burgundy Berry Pie, 122
Cream Cheese Cake, 63
Cream Cheese Swirl Brownies, 154
Cream of Tartar Biscuits, 180
Crisp, Blueberry Oatmeal, 179
Custard & Cream Pies, 129
Chocolate-Rum Chiffon Pie, 134
Coconut-Banana Cream Pie, 130
Coffee Cream Pie with Chocolate Crust,
136
Cranberry-Walnut Chess Pie, 131
Date Delight, 140
Irish Potato Pie, 137
Lemon Meringue Pie, 139
Lemon Sponge Pie, 135
Pecan Custard Pie, 133
Pumpkin-Butterscotch Mousse Pie, 132
Pumpkin Pie, 141
Sweet Potato Pecan Pie, 138
Sweet Potato Pie, Southern, 142

Danish Nut Loaf, 50
date(s)

Date and Walnut Cake, 67
Date Bran Muffins, 40
Date Delight, 140
Decadent Brownies, 148
Delicious Rhubarb Pie, 118
Dinner Rolls, 30
Downeast Burgundy Berry Pie, 122
Dumplings, Apple, 175

Easter Bread, Italian, 34
Empire Biscuits, 157

Festivals
Appalachian Fair, Gray, Tennessee, 78, 184
Arizona State Fair, Phoenix, Arizona, 94,
170, 181
California Exposition and State Fair,
Sacramento, California, 163, 181
Canfield Fair, Canfield, Ohio, 21, 24, 50,
118, 135, 152, 183
Central Maine Egg Festival, Pittsfield,
Maine, 102, 182
Champlain Valley Fair and Exposition,
Essex Junction, Vermont, 32, 76, 184
Colorado State Fair, Pueblo, Colorado,
53, 71, 181
Cranberry Harvest Festival, East Wareham,
Massachusetts, 37, 131, 156, 182
Delaware State Fair, Harrington,
Delaware, 106, 181
Dutchess County Fair, Rhinebeck,
New York, 17, 26, 36, 162, 183
Franklin County Fair, Greenfield,
Massachusetts, 145, 182
Fryeburg Fair, Fryeburg, Maine, 117, 182
Georgia National Fair, Perry, Georgia, 19,
130, 148, 154, 181
Great Gourd Bake-off, Keene, New
Hampshire, 144, 183
Great New England Food Festival,
Boston, Massachusetts, 43, 68, 100, 136
Hunterdon County 4-H and Agricultural
Fair, Flemington, New Jersey, 16, 39,
65, 92, 146, 183

Indiana State Fair, Indianapolis, Indiana, 31, 97, 160, 182

Iowa State Fair, Des Moines, Iowa, 157, 182

Louisiana Pecan Festival, Colfax, Louisiana, 99, 133, 182

Machias Wild Blueberry Festival, Machias, Maine, 122, 182

Michigan State Fair, Detroit, Michigan, 103, 165, 168, 182

Minnesota State Fair, St. Paul, Minnesota, 30, 54, 56, 82, 183

Morton Pumpkin Festival, Morton, Illinois, 132, 182

National Cherry Festival, Traverse City, Michigan, 41, 55, 107, 182

National Date Festival, Indio, California, 40, 67, 140, 181

National Peanut Festival, Dothan, Alabama, 74, 181

National Pie Championship, Lake Forest, Illinois, 115, 181

North Carolina Yam Festival, Tabor City, North Carolina, 138, 151, 183

Ohio State Fair, Columbus, Ohio, 108, 153, 183

Oklahoma State Fair, Oklahoma City, Oklahoma, 44, 84, 183

Old Farmer's Almanac Recipe Contest, The, Dublin, New Hampshire, 20, 25, 52, 58, 62, 95, 120, 125, 137, 139, 149, 159, 161, 164, 166, 183

Oregon State Fair and Expo, Salem, Oregon, 98, 123, 184

Ozark Empire Fair, Springfield, Missouri, 13, 80, 116, 147, 183

Peach Jamboree and Rodeo, Stonewall, Texas, 121, 184

Salem Fair, Salem, Virginia, 124, 184

Sandwich Fair, Center Sandwich, New Hampshire, 158, 183

Shelburne Grange Fair, Shelburne, Massachusetts, 66, 182

Springfield Filbert Festival, Springfield, Oregon, 72, 184

State Fair of Texas, Dallas, Texas, 22, 104, 134, 150, 184

Vermont Dairy Festival, Enosburg Falls, Vermont, 96, 184

Washington County Fair, Saunderstown, Rhode Island, 38, 184

Western Washington Fair, Puyallup, Washington, 28, 126, 184

Wheat Festival, Wellington, Kansas, 42, 167, 182

Wisconsin State Fair, West Allis, Wisconsin, 63, 184

Forest Chiffon Cake, 71

Frosted Cakes, 61
Apple-Walnut Celebration Cake, 87
Black Walnut Layer Cake, 80
Carrot Cake, The Best, Ever, 85
Chocolate Birthday Cake, The Best, 88
Chocolate Coconut Cream Cake, 82
Chocolate Torte with Vanilla Sauce and Raspberries, 68
Cream Cheese Cake, 63
Date and Walnut Cake, 67
Forest Chiffon Cake, 71
Hungarian Nut Torte, 62
Linzertorte Cake, 76
Moist Chocolate Cake with Cocoa Butter Frosting, 65
Nany's Caramel Peanut Butter Cake, 74
Peanut Butter Chocolate Chip Cupcakes, 66
Pumpkin Cake, 84
Swiss Chocolate Cake, 72
White Cake with Coconut and Whipped Cream, 78
Zucchini-Yogurt Cake, 90

Fruit Pies, 113
All-American Apple Pie, 124
Angie's Apple Crumb Pie, 120
Blueberry Streusel Pie, 116
Cherry Pie, 126
Cranberry Pie, 127
Delicious Rhubarb Pie, 118
Downeast Burgundy Berry Pie, 122

Fruit Pies *(continued)*
    Ginger Peach Pie, 128
    Great American Apple Pie, A, 115
    Peach Pie, 121
    Pear-Almond Pie, 123
    Schnappsy Peach Pie, 125
    Wild Blueberry Pie, 117

German Apple Pancakes, 176
German Hazelnut Cookies, 164
ginger
    Cranberry-Ginger Bread, 37
    Gingerbread Cake, 86
    Ginger Peach Pie, 128
    Old-Fashioned Gingerbread, 108
Golden Pumpkin Raisin Bread, 25
Grandma's Best Butter Cookies, 168
Great American Apple Pie, A, 115
Great-Grandmother's Banana Bread, 45
Greek Anise Bread, 24

Honey Oatmeal Bread, 31
Honey Whole-Wheat Bread, 16
Hungarian Nut Torte, 62

Irish Bread, 38
Irish Potato Pie, 137
Irish Soda Bread, 46
Italian Easter Bread, 34

Judging Scorecards, 13

Lemon(s)
    Blue Ribbon Tip, 101
    Lemon Meringue Pie, 139
    Lemon Sponge Pie, 135
    Lemony Hazelnut Bars, 145
Linzertorte Cake, 76

Michigan Cherry Muffins, 41
Moist Chocolate Cake with Cocoa Butter
   Frosting, 65
Molasses Cookies, 163
Muffins. *See* **Quick Breads & Muffins**

Nany's Caramel Peanut Butter Cake, 74
nut(s)
    Apple-Walnut Poppy Seed Coffeecake, 52
    Apricot-Almond Bars, 149
    Banana Nut Bread, 44
    Black Walnut Layer Cake, 80
    Blue Ribbon Tip, 73, 81, 99
    Caramel Rocky Road Bars, 150
    Chocolate Caramel-Pecan Cheesecake,
      103
    Cranberry-Walnut Chess Pie, 131
    Danish Nut Loaf, 50
    Date and Walnut Cake, 67
    Forest Chiffon Cake, 71
    German Hazelnut Cookies, 164
    Hungarian Nut Torte, 62
    Lemony Hazelnut Bars, 145
    Linzertorte Cake, 76
    Nany's Caramel Peanut Butter Cake, 74
    Orange Nut Bread with Orange Cream
      Cheese Spread, 43
    Peanut Butter Bars, 147
    Peanut Butter Chocolate Chip Cupcakes,
      66
    Pear-Almond Pie, 123
    Pecan Custard Pie, 133
    Plantation Pecan Cake, 99
    Sweet Potato Pecan Pie, 138
    Triple-Peanut Cookies, 158
    Triple-Treat Peanut Butter Chocolate
      Chip Cookies, 165

Oat(s)
    Blueberry Oatmeal Crisp, 179
    Honey Oatmeal Bread, 31
    Triple-Good Bars, 146
    Yam-Oatmeal Squares, 151
Old-Fashioned Gingerbread, 108
Old-Fashioned Potato Bread, 20
onion(s)
    Onion Lovers' Bread, 22
    Sourdough Onion-Potato Rye Bread
      with Caraway, 26
orange(s)

Chocolate-Orange Delights, 159
Cranberry-Orange Scones, 36
Orange Bowknot Rolls, 54
Orange Bread, 32
Orange Chiffon Cake, 94
Orange Citrus Cookies, 170
Orange Nut Bread with Orange Cream
    Cheese Spread, 43
Raspberry-Orange Mazurkas, 166

Pancakes, German Apple, 176
peach(es)
    Blue Ribbon Tip, 95
    Cowboy Cobbler, 95
    Peach Pie, 121
    Schnappsy Peach Pie, 125
Peanut Butter Bars, 147
Peanut Butter Chocolate Chip Cupcakes, 66
pear(s)
    Cranberry and Pear Butter Crumb Cake,
      100
    Pearadise Tart, 98
    Pear-Almond Pie, 123
Pecan Custard Pie, 133
pepper
    Blue Ribbon Tip, 39
    Cheddar Cheese Pepper Bread, 39
peppermint
    Chocolate Peppermint Creams, 161
Perfect Pound Cake, 97
Pies. *See* Custard & Cream Pies; Fruit Pies
pineapple(s)
    Pineapple Cheesecake, 102
Pizza, Zucchini, 177
Plantation Pecan Cake, 99
poppy seed(s)
    Apple-Walnut Poppy Seed Coffeecake, 52
    Buttermilk Poppy Seed Cake, 96
potato(es)
    Irish Potato Pie, 137
    Old-Fashioned Potato Bread, 20
    Sourdough Onion-Potato Rye Bread
      with Caraway, 26
Pudding, Blueberry Bread, 174

pumpkin(s)
    Golden Pumpkin Raisin Bread, 25
    Pumpkin-Butterscotch Mousse Pie, 132
    Pumpkin Cake, 84
    Pumpkin Cheesecake Bars, 144
    Pumpkin Pie, 141

Quick Breads & Muffins, 35
    Banana Bread, Great-Grandmother's, 45
    Banana Nut Bread, 44
    Cheddar Cheese Pepper Bread, 39
    Corn Bread, Skillet, 47
    Cranberry-Ginger Bread, 37
    Cranberry-Orange Scones, 36
    Date Bran Muffins, 40
    Irish Bread, 38
    Irish Soda Bread, 46
    Michigan Cherry Muffins, 41
    Orange Nut Bread with Orange Cream
      Cheese Spread, 43
    Spiced Pear Muffins, 48
    Zucchini Bread, 42

Raisin(s)
    Golden Pumpkin Raisin Bread, 25
    Irish Bread, 38
    Triple-Good Bars, 146
raspberry(ies)
    Chocolate Torte with Vanilla Sauce and
      Raspberries, 68
    Empire Biscuits, 157
    Raspberry-Lemon Pudding Cake, 109
    Raspberry-Orange Mazurkas, 166
rhubarb
    Delicious Rhubarb Pie, 118
Rolls. *See* Yeast Bread & Rolls
rum
    Chocolate-Rum Chiffon Pie, 134
rye bread
    Blue Ribbon Tip, 29
    Rye Bread, 28
    Sourdough Onion-Potato Rye Bread
      with Caraway, 26

Schnappsy Peach Pie, 125
Sima's Yummy Rugelach, 162
Skillet Corn Bread, 47
Sour Cream Coffeecake, 53, 59
Sourdough Onion-Potato Rye Bread with
    Caraway, 26
Spiced Pear Muffins, 48
sweet potato(es)
    Sweet Potato Pecan Pie, 138
    Sweet Potato Pie, Southern, 142
    Yam-Oatmeal Squares, 151
Swiss Chocolate Cake, 72

Toffee
    Apple-Toffee Cookies, 160
    Cranberry-Coconut Cookies with Toffee,
        156
Triple-Good Bars, 146
Triple-Peanut Cookies, 158
Triple-Treat Peanut Butter Chocolate Chip
    Cookies, 165

Unfrosted Cakes, 91
    Angel Food Cake, 104
    Banana Marble Pound Cake, 106
    Buttermilk Cake, Quick, 110
    Buttermilk Poppy Seed Cake, 96
    Cherry Pudding Cake, 107
    Chocolate Caramel-Pecan Cheesecake,
        103
    Coconut Cake, 92
    Cowboy Cobbler, 95
    Cranberry and Pear Butter Crumb Cake,
        100
    Old-Fashioned Gingerbread, 108
    Orange Chiffon Cake, 94
    Pearadise Tart, 98
    Perfect Pound Cake, 97
    Pineapple Cheesecake, 102
    Plantation Pecan Cake, 99
    Raspberry-Lemon Pudding Cake, 109
    World's Best Cheesecake, The, 112

Vanilla
    Chocolate Torte with Vanilla Sauce and
        Raspberries, 68

Wheat Germ Herb Bread, 21
White Bread, 17
White Cake with Coconut and Whipped
    Cream, 78
White Chip Chocolate Cookies, 167
Wild Blueberry Pie, 117
World's Best Brownies, The, 152
World's Best Cheesecake, The, 112

Yam(s). *See* sweet potato(es)
    Yam-Oatmeal Squares, 150
Yeast Breads & Rolls, 15
    Cornmeal Yeast Rolls, 19
    Dinner Rolls, 30
    Golden Pumpkin Raisin Bread, 25
    Greek Anise Bread, 24
    Honey Oatmeal Bread, 31
    Honey Whole-Wheat Bread, 16
    Italian Easter Bread, 34
    Old-Fashioned Potato Bread, 20
    Onion Lovers' Bread, 22
    Orange Bread, 32
    Rye Bread, 28
    Sourdough Onion-Potato Rye Bread
        with Caraway, 26
    Wheat Germ Herb Bread, 21
    White Bread, 17

Zucchini
    Zucchini Bread, 42
    Zucchini Drop Cookies, 172
    Zucchini Pizza, 177
    Zucchini-Yogurt Cake, 90